I0181301

To my father, Jim, who has been, and will remain, the greatest
Coach a son could ask for, both on and off the court.

CHAPTER 1

The gym smelled of sweat, wood, old leather and a hint of mothballs or dust. Kevin took a deep breath, the crisp air stinging his lungs. He loved that smell. He missed that smell. It reminded him of home.

He missed how home used to be.

It was 5:30 on a cool November morning and nearly pitch dark in Covenant Prep High School's Stottlemyer Arena, the only light coming from the rising sun slipping through the windows on the east side of the gym. It was just the way Kevin liked the court these days. He relished the solitude, where there were no questions about Dad, about college.

He kept the hood of his light gray and royal blue Prep sweatshirt snug around his head as he jogged up and down, shaking the sleep out of his legs, the yawns out of his lungs. His legs were fresh from the off-season, free of the aches and bruises that would be sure to come by the end of the year. It was still cold enough where he could see his breath hang in the air for a split second, like steam rising from a pot.

He grabbed a ball from the rack on the sidelines, so beaten up the lettering had faded into indecipherable leather hieroglyphics, and began pounding it, crossing over every few steps as he jogged and his legs got looser, his mind a little less foggy. The sound of leather smacking wood echoed softly off the creaky old bleachers, which were pulled up tightly against the walls. This was the sound of his childhood.

He thought of tomorrow, the season-opener against St. Andrew's, their cross-town rivals and last year's state champs, and he ran faster, pounded harder. This would be his last season at Covenant Prep. He had been told, several times in fact, that if he improved here, got better there, the Stags were sure bets to supplant those Lions atop the standings.

Still his game hadn't been the same without Coach.

Soon the shots began flying; 1,000 of them. This was his routine, every day. That's how many Coach said to take, and that's how many Kevin would be taking each morning for the remainder of the season. Fifty mid-range jumpers from the left wing, 50 from the right, 100 full-court layups using his right hand only, 100 full-court layups using his left hand only. Little droplets of sweat began zig-zagging down his cheeks. He missed that, too.

Coach also gave him another tip—work on your 3-pointers. Standing 5-foot-10 and weighing 175 pounds, Kevin wasn't going to carve up future college defenses darting through the inside as he'd done at will in high school. He needed to polish his distance game. So he began from deep—30 threes from the right, 30 from the top, 30 from the left. More full-court layups. Sweat was now pouring, puddling onto his chest, darkening his once-icy gray sweatshirt to the sinister color of a storm cloud. Only then did he take it off and toss it to the sideline. The cool air of the gym felt nice on his overheated body.

Another 3-pointer hung in the air, sure to go in, when he heard her voice.

"That's not gonna go innnnnnn," it rang out in a disinterested tone. The shot clanged off the front of the rim.

Of course, she was here. She was always here. It would have been naïve to expect any less.

"We gonna do this again, Lyla?" Kevin said tiredly, almost a sigh, not looking towards the girl with the sun-kissed hair and magnificent blue eyes standing by the door.

"Would you look at that, you missed," she answered, blowing her gum into a bubble and popping it with a sharp 'POP.' "Just like you did with those two free throws last year."

Kevin winced.

"Oh, I'm sorry. Too soon?"

Kevin retrieved his ball from where the rim had sent it bouncing. He didn't look at her.

"So we are going to do this again this year, then?"

She didn't answer. Lyla, wearing the same Covenant Prep sweatshirt and the same black sweatpants Kevin had on, grabbed a ball off the rack and began walking over to the hoop on the other side of the court.

"I'm using that hoop too, you know," Kevin called.

"It's had enough misses already," she said, maintaining her disinterested tone. "Don't worry. I'll fix it right up for you."

Kevin shook his head. He wished she weren't so good. He glanced at her end of the court, and his eyes found the placard posted above the door, the one with the school records posted on them.

Most points in a game: Lyla Storm, 58, 2012

Most career points: Lyla Storm, 1,800, 2010-present

Most 3-pointers in a game: Lyla Storm, 14, 2012

It went on. Lyla had been the best player at Covenant Prep for the past three years. Every record, aside from the rebounding and steals categories, had her name next to it. She even invented a few program firsts that wouldn't be listed on any placard: first triple-double, first quadruple-double, first player to score 40 points in a game, first player to score more than the entire opposing team, first player to be offered a scholarship as a freshman.

Kevin could hear the 'shhhtck, shhhtck, shhhtck' coming every few seconds from Lyla swishing shot after shot. His 3-pointers rattled in and out; hers fell through like water.

An hour passed.

"So, how bad are y'all," she eventually said, "gonna get your butts handed to you by St. Andrew's tomorrow?"

"What's it to you?" Kevin panted, looking over. She too had ditched her sweatshirt, revealing a lipstick pink tank top that was slowly turning a wine red from her sweat. Her long, tan arms were glistening but there was no eyeliner bleeding down her face or smeared lipstick. Lyla never wore makeup. Never had to.

"Oh, trust me, I don't care," she snorted, popping her gum twice more. "There's just a running bet among us girls that you might lose by more points than we score. I couldn't take the bet, of course, because I don't want to have to stop scoring to win some bet."

Kevin eyed her curiously, pondering how it was possible to pack so much hubris into such a petite frame.

"You two getting along this year?" came a voice by the door. Lyla dropped her smug look and replaced it with a genuine smile. Kevin knew of only two people who could draw that smile—real, heartfelt—on Lyla Storm, and one of them was towering in the doorframe.

"Coach Koontz!" Lyla squealed excitedly.

"Ma'am," Kevin nodded.

As Kevin's and Lyla's were, Coach Koontz's long legs were clad in sweatpants, though her pair was red with a blue Stag, Covenant Prep's mascot, down the right side. She was abnormally tall for a woman, towering a good six inches above Kevin, and she ate up enormous swaths of court with each stride. Her coffee-colored ponytail swished behind her as she walked with the noticeable swagger of a former collegiate athlete. Kevin couldn't help but feel a pang of attraction for the woman, who met the pair at midcourt and was immediately being wrapped up in Lyla's arms.

"Aw, c'mon you're so sweaty," Koontz said, feigning disgust, throwing her hands up, mouth twisting like she had just eaten something sour. "How long have the two of you been here? Since the crack of dawn, I suppose?"

"Made four-hundred shots, coach," Lyla bragged, smiling her toothpaste-commercial smile.

"Good, now save some for St. Andrew's tomorrow. That goes for you, too," she said, looking sternly at Kevin. "That Miller boy is back. Heard he committed to Duke, too. You're going to have to stick him, you know. Future Blue Devil. Won't be easy."

"Now quick," she said, glancing at the neon green watch wrapped around her left wrist, "the bell is going to ring any minute now and you two are not going to class smelling like pigs. Get showered and dressed and get your gross butts to class."

Lyla flipped her basketball into the crate as if she were shooting a jump shot. It went in. Of course it went in. She shot a haughty look at Kevin, scooped up her sweatshirt and jogged to the locker room. Kevin felt his eyes following her long legs as she sauntered out. Koontz sighed. She had been watching her too.

"What am I going to do with that cocky little princess?"

"Win another championship, I guess," Kevin muttered. And then he walked, head down, to his own locker room.

Just before he could reach the door, Koontz cleared her throat, paused, and posed one more question.

"Kevin."

She said this slowly, measuring her tone, choosing her words carefully. "How's your father?"

His eyes found the floor. They always did that when it came to speaking about his dad, when it came to Coach. He looked up, shook his head and walked out.

CHAPTER 2

Jared had no idea what time it was when his eyes finally opened on Tuesday morning. Sunlight was flooding into his window. Far too much sunlight. Chances were, it was well past 8 o'clock. He needed to be at school by 7:45.

"Shit."

He pulled himself up so he was in a sitting position on the couch and discovered he was naked save for the faded pair of brown boxer briefs around his waist. He took stock of his surroundings. The smell of stale beer and Cheetos and old cigarettes filled his nose; it made him want to vomit. He didn't. This was an odor he was fairly accustomed to beginning his day with. He glanced at the coffee table, crowded with empty and half-drank beer cans and stained checks from the Air Force that his brother, Steve, had sent home from Afghanistan. Jared knew he should probably get moving, but motivation wasn't coming just yet, even if it were game day.

St. Andrew's? Was that who they played? He wasn't sure. He burped, and the taste of partly digested beer filled his mouth. He nearly vomited again.

Stumbling, body still fighting the effects of last night's party—though was it technically a party even if it were just him and three girls? —Jared glanced around for a shirt and pants; they had to be around somewhere. His flannel button-down had somehow found a resting place on his kitchen counter, his sweatpants next to the fridge. Players were supposed to wear a shirt and tie to school on game days. Oh well. He chose to abide by the theory that it only mattered if he had his jersey come game-time.

Jared fumbled through the bare cabinets, finding a jar of peanut butter and a spoon, and shoveled a few globs into his mouth, swigging the remnants of a warm, day-old Budweiser to chase it down. Breakfast.

Then he slinked outside, shielding his bloodshot eyes from the sun as if he were saluting it, and slipped into his truck, rusted to the point that its once vibrant red exterior resembled clay, and drove off to Prep.

"Are you kiddin' me? First game of the year and this is what you're trying to pull?"

Jared didn't respond, standing silently in front of his coach, Jack Snyder, eyes focused on anything but the man glaring at him. Coach Snyder's short-cropped black hair was tucked under a gray hat with blue lettering that read 'PREP' with the school's red stag on the side. Jared could tell that he was attempting to burn holes through him with his stony gaze, the way coaches do when trying to intimidate players without the use of words. Jared smiled back.

Coach Stottlemyer, Kevin's father, Prep's coach for the past decade, never allowed this type of behavior. Threw Jared out the first day of practice three years ago, when Jared showed up half-cocked on vodka, one of his brother's many brilliant ideas. It would ease the nerves, he said. It would be fine, he said. Jared owed Coach 50 suicides. That morning, he did puke. This morning he held it down, and this new coach, Coach Snyder, certainly wasn't going to make him do it. Jared glanced at the unpacked boxes surrounding Snyder's desk. Aside from a radio, which was on a commercial break—Greenmount Station was serving half-off apps for a Prep win! —Snyder still hadn't settled in much, which, in Jared's mind, meant he hadn't been properly tested yet.

"Coach," Jared mumbled, "can you just sign the thing?"

He noticed the way Snyder perked up when he said "coach." This was Snyder's first head coaching gig, which was no small deal in the town of Gaithersburg. This was a town where the head basketball coach signed autographs, kisses babies, posed for pictures, received 50 percent off meals wherever he went, and even those tabs were often picked up by the locals. The radio cackled on Snyder's desk, evidently back from the commercial. He had been about to say something, but he paused.

"St. Andrew's tonight, Rob. Who you taking?"

"I mean, you have to go with St. Andrew's, right? State champs, bringing back Jack Miller. And that kid is the real deal, Scott. Going to Duke, you know? That's a good ballplayer. And with Prep, we've just got so many question marks, you know? We don't know how the Stottlemyer boy is going to handle last year's collapse in the championship, and we don't know much about the new coach, Jack Snyder. I mean, this guy has never been a head coach, you know? And to take over for Covenant Prep as your first gig? Those are some big shoes, man, some big, big shoes. I can't remember the last time we hired a guy fresh off an assistant job. I've never met the dude. Maybe he's great, you know? But none of these boys have seen a team coached by anybody but Bill Stottlemyer. So we don't know. That's the main thing: We don't know. We'll see tonight how everybody handles this thing, but I can't say we should expect much."

Snyder flipped the radio off and glanced down at the paper Jared had placed on the table. Jared had a strong feeling the coach would sign the faux note, which would dismiss his tardiness—an offense punishable by sitting out a game—as a doctor's appointment. Snyder picked up a pen and paused. He took a long, measured look at Jared and back to the paper again. He chewed his bottom lip and furrowed his eyebrows. What would it say about him if he sat the team's best player in his first game on the job? This was not how he wanted to begin his first season. If Snyder wanted to win, he couldn't afford to sit Jared, the team's leading scorer from last season, especially against St. Andrew's, especially in the season opener.

"I tell you what I'm gonna do," Coach Snyder began. He put pen to paper. "I'm gonna sign this paper, risking my job before we've played our very first game, and you're gonna give me the best damn game of your life, you hear me?"

The corners of Jared's mouth twitched upwards a tick.

"And then, after you drop thirty on St. Andrew's tonight, you're gonna give me twenty suicides. Do I make myself clear?"

"Crystal, sir."

Jared fought back a yawn. In that same moment, he decided he would not run a single one of those suicides.

"Good."

Jared swiped the forged note and turned to leave, but before he could, Coach Snyder grabbed him by the arm and yanked him back so the two were nose-to-nose, like a baseball manager and an umpire after an awful call. They were so close that Jared could smell the coffee on his coach's breath.

"And I tell you what, this is the last gosh darn doctor's note I sign for you, boy. And don't think I couldn't smell that alcohol on you from the parking lot. Get a shower and get to class."

Jared, still inches from Coach Snyder, brushed his shaggy hair out of his face and walked out.

At 2:30, the bell rang three times. Jared awoke from his stealthy nap in biology and smiled. School was blessedly over.

In the science quad, Kevin's stomach dropped, that feeling you get on a roller coaster when it plummets back to earth.

In the auxiliary gym, Lyla slammed a stack of quizzes she was grading for Coach Koontz and raised her arms to the sky.

It was almost game time.

Kevin walked, zombie-like, to his locker. He could make out the sounds of students wishing him luck, but could hear nothing specific.

This would be just his second game without Coach. The first hadn't gone particularly well.

When he arrived at his locker, Kevin found the familiar sight of a red poster with "GO KEVIN! BEAT ST. ANDREWS!" written in perfect handwriting. There would be a poster like this every single game for the rest of the season. His stomach sank further. Mandy. He didn't think he could physically handle her right now.

"Hey baby!" she squealed.

She was as reliable as the sunrise, that girl. Mandy didn't miss a single game last year, not when she had the flu, not when

Kevin was suspended for fighting with Jared in practice, not even when the rest of the cheerleaders didn't travel to an away game, so she drove, and her car broke down and she had to walk the last half mile in the snow just to catch the second half.

Kevin shut his eyes and took a deep breath.

Mandy bounded down the hall, her shock of cherry curls bouncing this way and that. She wore jeans and her blue cheerleading top with the red 'P' in the middle, which matched her vibrantly red lipstick and naturally rosy cheeks. Kevin's hands found a brownie Mandy had baked him and left in his locker for him earlier that day. He popped the entire thing in his mouth.

"You nervous?" she said, kissing him on the cheek.

"Course," he mumbled through the mountain of chocolate.

"Good," she said, running her hands through his hair. "That just means you care. Wish I could stay longer, but I gotta get the girls ready. Good luck, good luck, good luck!"

He nodded.

She kissed him on the cheek again, turned on her heels and was bounding off. Kevin sighed.

Kevin wasn't sure how long Lyla had been standing at her locker, three down from his.

"You know what day it is?" she crooned.

Kevin didn't bother to respond. He looked down, fingers seeking another brownie.

"It's Lyla Stormmmmmm dayyyyyyyy! Hope you bought tickets."

She brushed past him, knocking Mandy's poster down as she passed. He rolled his eyes. There were a lot of things in life that did not make sense to Kevin: physics, electricity, choosing wrestling over basketball. Lyla Storm was right among them.

CHAPTER 3

Everything was right.

Stottlemyer Arena's 1,500-seat capacity was filled with ostensibly every citizen in Gaithersburg. The boys in the student section wore Prep's signature royal blue, the girls donned their reds, turning the gym into a rollicking sea of reds and blues and teenage exuberance.

Kevin could hear the chants from inside the locker room, the same ones that normally stretched the corners of his mouth into a smile, that got his heart beating like a war drum.

Which was why everything was wrong.

Before games, Kevin was invariably a nervous wreck. He chiseled his fingernails to stubs during class. He bit his lower lip until the metallic taste of blood trickled down his throat. He tapped his toes and cracked his knuckles. Sometimes he puked. Nerves were good, though. Nerves meant he cared. That's what Coach said. That's what Mandy said.

But now, 20 minutes before tipoff, there were no nerves. His palms weren't damp with sweat. The usual butterflies weren't fluttering about his uneasy stomach. Instead, that stomach was home to an icy pit of impending dread. The last time he had taken the court without Coach on the sidelines, Kevin missed two free throws with no time left in the state championship. At that point in the season, Kevin had been shooting 85 percent from the line. He was as much of a sure thing as there was in high school basketball. One would have tied it and sent it to overtime. Two would have won it. Kevin was going to be a hero. But the first rimmed out. Instinctively, he had glanced to the sideline where Coach would have been standing, where he had been standing at every game since Kevin was in fifth grade, sharply dressed in a pinstripe suit. Yet Coach hadn't been there. He was in a hospital, under the careful knife of a surgeon, and Kevin was playing—no, Kevin was losing—a game. Without Coach to fix his shot, Kevin knew with a horrible certainty he wouldn't make the second, and he didn't, listening to it clang off the rim, hearing the explosion from St. Andrew's as they rushed the court in delirious celebration.

Now, the dread was back, marinating in that arctic pit where his heart should be. Now, Kevin was listening to the foreign speech of Coach Snyder, who was imploring his players in bellows and roars to get excited.

"They don't deserve to be on our court!" he yelled.

Jared snorted. Kevin's eyes found his shoes. What a horrible speech.

"Let's take it to 'em!"

The dread worsened, the pit expanded. Kevin was lost before the referee even tossed the jump ball. He fumbled a pass from Brandon Thompson on the first play and it squirted out of bounds. He missed an open jumper two plays later and was duped by a Jack Miller crossover so bad he nearly fell.

"Are you kiddin' me, Stottlemyer?" Coach Snyder screamed. "You know what, get out, let me get somebody in there who is gonna show a little effort."

Just like that, after two minutes of what had promised to be an indelibly successful season, Kevin was sent to the bench to mull over his two turnovers, missed shot and absence of defense. He should have been livid. He was relieved.

Jared kept the Stags afloat. A twisting jumper in the lane made it 10-7, a steal and fast break dunk 14-11, but with Kevin out, nobody had a chance at stopping Jack Miller.

Jared was tall and rangy, standing 6-foot-3 with arms that stretched nearly to his knees, but he wasn't nearly as fast as Kevin and didn't have the lateral speed that could contain St. Andrew's' star. By the end of the first quarter, Prep trailed 20-15. Miller had scored 14.

Kevin picked himself off the end of the bench and joined his team in a circle as Snyder prepped them for the second quarter. Jared grabbed a fistful of his jersey and yanked him so that they were nose to nose.

"What planet you on right now, huh?" Jared growled. Kevin thought he could still smell a little alcohol on his teammate's breath. "You gonna play or what?"

Coach Snyder looked up from his mini-drawing board and said nothing, perhaps unsure of how to react to two teammates, the best two players from last year's runner-up championship squad, feuding after one quarter on the job.

"Just get out of my face, man," Kevin mumbled, shaking himself free of Jared's grasp.

"Pansy, that's what you are," Jared sneered. "Stay on the bench then. We'll do it without you."

The buzzer sounded. Kevin slinked back to the bench. Coach Snyder said nothing. Jared continued pouring in points, and the crowd responded in kind, chanting his name after each 3-pointer ripped through the net. Still, nobody could stop Miller.

He was quicksilver fast with a deadly first step and a crossover smooth as butter. He carved through the lane for layups, stepped back for threes, dished to wide-open teammates under the basket.

It was a one-on-one match between Jared and Miller, and despite all of Jared's offensive firepower, he couldn't keep up. By half, Prep trailed by 17. Kevin hadn't seen the court since he was first taken out.

In the locker room, Jared rocketed a chair into the showers, and the only sound in the room for about a minute was the empty echoing of metal on metal and the soft panting of 12 defeated and frustrated basketball players.

"I don't know what that was," hissed Snyder, "but it sure as hell wasn't basketball. I tell you what, I didn't take this job to be quit on by a bunch of pansies in the first sixteen minutes. No, I did not. I came to coach a bunch of winners like I know you are. That's what I came for. So get your act together and let's kick some ass."

The speech didn't work. Miller reigned unstoppable. Kevin returned for five minutes in the third quarter, scoring four points and turning it over two more times. When Brandon checked in for him again, he wasn't sure he had ever felt so relieved in his life.

Jared was utterly exhausted, having played every second through the first three quarters, and soon his shots were falling short as the waning strength in his legs betrayed him. He had put together a spectacular display of basketball, dropping in 28 points and grabbing 14 rebounds, but it was too much to demand of one player to carry an entire team.

Prep lost 71-56. Miller hung 40 on them. Even the Prep crowd, normally a raucously hostile bunch, was impressed with the future Duke Blue Devil. Kevin sank his teeth into a towel to keep from crying. The tears wouldn't have been for his performance or the team losing its home season opener. He just wanted Coach back.

Mandy, all smiles on her lips but worry in her eyes, tried to grab Kevin as he walked, head down, to the locker room, but he shook her off.

Kevin wouldn't remember what Coach Snyder would say in the locker room next, something about a rough start, a great game by Jared, and a reference to Rome not being built in a day. The only thing Kevin could recall from that locker room was that, for the first time since he had picked up a basketball at the age of 3, he did not care about the game of basketball. For the first time, Kevin wanted to quit.

Somewhere dark. That's what Kevin needed. He drew the hood of his gray sweatshirt tight around his head in hopes no students or parents or even Mandy would recognize him and he collapsed into a corner of the visiting bleachers.

The bleachers had cleared substantially with the boys game over and the girls set to play, but a good number remained. The end result was almost predetermined. Prep's girls hadn't lost a game in two years. With Lyla Storm running the show, they were the epitome of the proverbial unstoppable force.

She had averaged 32 points per game last year as the Lady Stags romped to a championship. St. Andrew's' girls were an awful excuse for a basketball team, which made it all the more obvious that the fans who had stuck around were there for either one of two reasons: they were parents watching their child, or they were there to watch Lyla Storm play ball. The latter half was mostly boys looking to earn some points with Prep's golden girl. Though they wouldn't dare admit it, even some of the parents were more interested in watching Lyla than their own daughter. Only two remained who did not care much about the Lady Stags or how many points Lyla scored.

Kevin spotted them across the gym and he sunk deeper into his corner, hoping they hadn't glimpsed him sneaking back in. But they had. They knew him too well not to recognize his quick stride and tendency to become a recluse after losses.

Jocelyn and Tim, his blessed, magnificent, eternally beatific kid sister and brother.

"Kev!" cried Tim, who was wearing a homemade jersey with Kevin's number 0 scrawled sloppily across the front in blue and red marker. "Don't worry about it, man! You'll get 'em next time! You will, I just know it! And Jared was awesome! Oh, man, if you had, like, played like you normally do, you'd have whooped some butt. Not that you didn't play like you normally do. I mean, you normally like kick super butt. But you still kicked butt."

"Right," Kevin mumbled.

Jocelyn, a precocious girl of nine who preferred to bury herself in books rather than sports, sensed Kevin's mood and plopped onto his lap, wrapping her pencil thin arms around his neck.

"It's alright," she said in voice so teensy you'd have thought it was a cartoon. "We still love you."

"Thanks, Joc," Kevin said, gingerly returning the hug. "Now go, you two. I gotta be alone. Go watch Lyla or something. She's probably better than I am right now."

And for the first time, Kevin actually believed that to be true.

Lyla lived up to the billing. Earlier that day the local paper, the *Gaithersburg Gazette*, rolled out a huge package on her, labeling her as the best girls player in Prep history, which was no small claim. She had made sure everybody read it, wagging it around between classes, showing everybody who cared, as well as those who didn't, at every available opportunity. People would call her arrogant if it weren't true.

She scooped up the jump ball and breezed down the court, the ball an extension of her hand the whole way. She zigged past one defender with a nifty through the legs crossover and spun back the other way to avoid another and casually laid it in.

2-0 Lyla over St. Andrew's.

Lyla picked off a pass on the ensuing possession and went coast-to-coast again, flying by the hopeless defenders.

Kevin sighed from his spot in the corner. He pulled his hood a little tighter. He would be hearing about this game in the morning. Lyla just kept going: a 3 from the corner, a pull up jumper from the foul line, another layup through traffic. By the end of the quarter Prep was up 22-3. Lyla had 16.

Coach Koontz didn't call the dogs off, either. Lyla played every minute of the remainder of the first half, running her total up to 30 points with just two missed shots.

By then, the crowd had all but disintegrated; they had seen what they had come to see. Lyla Storm was better than ever. The newspaper story, as glowing as it read, had somehow undersold her abilities.

Coach Koontz subbed her out with four minutes left in the third quarter. Lyla knew her day was finished—41 points, 6 assists, 0 turnovers. As always, she was subbed out by Tara French, an awkward girl who was an extension of Lyla's hip. The quicker Lyla scored, the more Tara played.

What was left of the sparse crowd rose and gave a standing ovation for Lyla. She basked in it, grinning widely and waving back. Then whistles and whoops for Tara followed and Lyla playfully slapped her on the butt.

"Go score twenty for me, sis!"

They weren't actually sisters but they may as well have been. They did everything together. When Tara didn't land a prom date the year before, Lyla ditched hers and the two went to the movies instead. Lyla's date was devastated; she didn't even let him know she wouldn't show. When Tara first moved in from New Jersey, Lyla was the one who sat next to the quirky girl with the pale skin, red hair, and freckles covering every visible inch of her body. They ate together every day from then on out, practically inseparable. As much as Tara tried to learn the game from Lyla, though, the girl was just not born to play basketball.

She tripped on her own feet on the first possession down the court, missed a shot so bad on the next that fans wondered aloud if it were a pass, and was so lost on defense she actually spun in a circle looking for her mark, who was busy making a layup. Kevin caught Coach Koontz covering her mouth to stifle a fit of giggles while Tara and the benchwarmers tried their darnedest. The game mercifully ended, both for St. Andrew's and the benchwarmers, five minutes later, and Kevin attempted a quick escape out of the gym. It wasn't quick enough.

"Told ya' you'd suck," Lyla crooned from the court. "See you tomorrow, loser."

Kevin pretended not to hear. A reporter and a photographer hurried across the court to catch Lyla.

Kevin pulled his hood tighter and continued walking until his lungs felt the cold air outside. It felt so nice he didn't stop when he reached his car, walking until the beads of sweat trickling down his face were frozen into tiny teardrops. It was then that he realized it: Stottlemyer Arena, the gym that bore his very last name, in honor of his father, the place that had once been his sanctuary, had begun to feel more like a prison.

Maryland Christian Athletic Conference Standings

Boys

St. Andrew's 1-0

Bishop O'Connell 1-0

Good Counsel 1-0

St. Anselm's 1-0

Covenant Prep 0-1

Bishop McNamara 0-1

Bishop Ireton 0-1

Gonzaga 0-1

Girls

Covenant Prep 1-0

Bishop O'Connell 1-0

Gonzaga 1-0

Good Counsel 1-0

St. Andrew's 0-1

St. Anselm's 0-1

Bishop Ireton 0-1

Bishop McNamara 0-1

CHAPTER 4

Kevin sat in his ancient Mercury Sable, now more rust than it was silver, engine turned off, listening only to the sound of his steady heartbeat—*thump-thump, thump-thump, thump-thump*. He closed his eyes, concentrating on feeling the blood pulsing through his temples—*thump-thump, thump-thump*—so he could think of anything else but the game, or basketball, or Coach. The sweat on his shirt had frozen, coating him in an icy layer. It was incredibly uncomfortable yet he still didn't want to go inside. Not yet. He couldn't face Coach, wasn't ready for the sight that haunted his dreams every single night and had him waking in tears every single morning.

He just sat, slumped in the driver's seat, breath hanging in the air like a ghost, fogging up the windshield until he could no longer see the streetlights twinkling in front of the house. Kevin took a deep breath. He had to go in.

He collapsed into his spot at the kitchen table, the one on the far left facing out of the window, looking over the back deck and to the woods beyond where he had played countless games of capture the flag. His mother, Carla, had laid out a heaping pile of spaghetti with four monstrous meatballs and a note scrawled in exquisitely neat handwriting on top.

"Rough game I hear. Couldn't make it, had to take care of dad. Come say hey before bed. Love u."

Kevin shoved the plate aside. The note made him sick. He buried his head in his hands. How long could he wait until he had to see Coach?

"Kev? That you?" a voice called from upstairs.

Not long enough. His mother had heard him. His heart sunk. He hated this part.

Kevin walked up the stairs, an obstacle course of barbies and GI Joes and trucks, and creaked open the door to his parents' room.

"Come in, hon." His mom's voice was impossibly sweet.

He walked in, keeping his head low.

"We lost," he mumbled, eyes finding the tan carpet.

"It's just one game, sweetie. You'll get 'em next time. Isn't that right, Bill?"

Kevin looked up, finding the man who was a shell of his former self.

Bill Stottlemyer lay propped up by a stack of pillows on the left side of the bed, IVs stuck into various parts of his arms and connected to humming machines where a night stand would have been, where a night stand had been for the first 16-plus years of Kevin's life.

His skin was a sickly gray, the color of a sky before a snowstorm, and his face was gaunt. His eyes, once a fierce green, were somehow dimmer, as if the sickness was leeching every possible semblance of life from the man.

"Not too great today, huh?" his father smiled and then wheezed. "Just one game, Kev. Happens."

Kevin shook his head, unable to speak. It's difficult to make an audible sound when a baseball-sized lump is seizing your throat.

"Only reason to work that much harder," his father said in his whispery, raspy voice. That was how he talked these days. "You'll be fine. I know you will. How'd Jared do? How was Coach Snyder?"

Kevin tried to manage a smile. It failed.

"Jared was good, the only reason we didn't lose by a hundred, actually. Coach Snyder, eh, I don't know what you see in that guy, pops. He sucks."

"Give him time."

Bill wheezed and coughed, a sign that Kevin knew meant the conversation was over. His dad only had so many words in him before the effort became too exhausting.

"I'm gonna jump in the shower."

Minutes later he was laying down in the shower. He never stood anymore, not since the day he heard of his father's diagnosis. He simply laid down and let the water wash over him. Maybe, he thought, it would wash away everything. Maybe it would take him back to when everyone was healthy and there wasn't a tumor ravaging his dad's brain. He closed his eyes, slapped a warm towel over his face, and thought back, as he always did, to the days when his father wasn't hooked up to the humming machines keeping him alive.

Bill Stottlemyer had been strong as thunder once. He still owned all the male scoring records at Prep, set some 30 years ago, and his silky jumper had earned him a full ride to Pittsburgh, his hometown school. There, he became a four-year All-American—the first in program history to do so—and went pro for a bit.

Bill, for all his successes at the amateur levels, wasn't built for the pro game. He was a 6-foot-4 tweener between shooting guard and small forward, without the shot needed to play shooting guard nor the strength needed to play small forward. He turned in a pretty unremarkable career in the big leagues, hopping from team to team, serving as a Band-Aid when injuries called for an extra bench player.

Bill was no fool. He knew his pro days weren't going to amount to much, so he called it a career after five seasons, due in large part to a striking blonde with emerald eyes named Carla he had met in Miami during a series there.

They wed in six months.

It was almost frightening how much Kevin emanated Bill's likeness, down to the matching birthmark on their neck—a red spot the size of an apple that looked like it was constantly sunburned.

When most kids were watching the Lion King and Aladdin, Kevin was flipping through his dad's old game film. In the third grade, Kevin's teacher asked him what he wanted to be when he grew up. He told her that he wanted to be just like his dad.

Basketball was all Bill had ever wanted to do. Basketball was all Kevin wanted to do. Bill coached every team Kevin ever played on, to the point that even off the court, Kevin called him Coach.

It's amazing what two words can change. Brain cancer. Knocks the wind right out of you. As cancers do, it had begun silently, as innocuous as a stutter. Just one year ago, Bill had been donning his suit and coaching Kevin and Jared and one heck of a Stags team.

Prep had been on a tear. It won its first 12 games and cruised past the defending champs, St. Andrew's, 68-43. Jared even quit drinking during season because even he couldn't bear to let Coach down.

Then, one day at practice, Coach had ordered Brandon Thompson to run a play called Duke. It was only a slight wrinkle from their normal shuffle offense: Instead of Kevin, the off-ball guard, making the first cut in their offense, Brandon, the ball-side guard, would.

Brandon ran it perfectly. Coach reamed him out.

"Did I not just say, 'Run Duke'?"

The players stood, bewildered.

"What's everyone standing around for? Run it again and run it right!" Coach bellowed.

"Uh, Coach?" Kevin had asked, confused and, admittedly, slightly amused. "That *was* Duke."

Coach paused for a second, mulling it over in his head. His wide shoulders, which had been tight with an angry tension, relaxed and he roared with laughter.

"Oh, boy, I'm sorry, Brandon. You're absolutely right! Must be getting old."

Everybody laughed. Soon, though, the laughs stopped.

Soon Coach was mixing up plays every practice. He was going to the grocery store, coming back hours later, lost because he had made a wrong turn and forgotten how to get back, once venturing out so far he came to in West Virginia. Then he was forgetting names and birthdays and games.

Each time, he blamed old age, a waning ability to concentrate, not eating enough fruits or veggies. Each time, he pretended not to hear his wife as she implored—no, begged—him to get checked out at the hospital. He was too stubborn for that.

This was a man who played half a basketball game with a broken foot, waving off the sub who had been sent to check in for the guy who could barely walk. Didn't matter. Bill was still scoring. He went on to hit the game winner that night. Then he went to the hospital.

So no, Bill would not go to the hospital for some memory issues. Everybody had them, right?

Then one day, it was not just his memory. He had been in his office, watching a game film when his left arm began tingling. His head felt funny. Then he collapsed. Paramedics rushed him to the hospital in time to determine Bill had suffered a stroke.

It was caused by a pea-sized tumor in his brain. Brain cancer. Had Bill come in earlier, the doctors may have been able to slow it, even beat it. Bill had ignored the early warning signs. The tumor had grown, spread. It was Grade III at least. It was more than likely going to take Bill's life before his 47th birthday.

Bill was not likely to see Kevin graduate from high school.

Brain cancer or not, Bill was still Bill. He took this news as if it were any other obstacle: a team throwing in a press he hadn't seen before, a defender playing box-and-one, a hostile crowd. He never viewed it as undefeatable. Impossible is nothing. That was his thing.

Nobody was to know why he stepped down, three days before the championship game last season. He simply didn't have the energy. Besides, the kids knew the plays better than he did. Better to groom a promising assistant for next year than to waste the biggest game of the year, the biggest game of most of the players' lives at that point, pretending to coach. He knew he was entirely worthless on the court.

Kevin never saw it like that. His dad always had the answer.

"Why did the defense know where I was about to pass it?"

"Because you telegraphed it, Kev. Look them off next time."

And he would.

"Why did that shot hit front rim?"

"Because you didn't use your legs, Kev. Release at the peak of your jump, not on the way down."

And the next one would drop.

"They're taking away our first cut, what do we have to do to get an open shot?"

"Run a backdoor cut, mix it up, keep the defense honest."

And Prep would almost always score on the following possession.

Kevin didn't have that without Coach. He didn't have his dad's fix in last year's championship game when he missed the first free throw that would have tied it. He knew there was no chance he would make the second.

The court had been Kevin's favorite place in the world, better than Disney World or the beach, snowy mountains or California, because he was with Coach, doing what they loved most. It was where he went when he failed a test. It was where he went when him and Mandy got in a fight. It was where he went when he told his mother he was going to the library. Without Coach, the court was eerie, different. Empty. He hated it, had never felt comfortable on it since.

The shower water had not been warm for some time. Kevin could have laid there for hours, basking in the darkness and the water, away from the near certain death that hung over his father's head. He flicked the knob with his foot and the water shut off. He shivered, goosebumps shooting up and down his body.

He had to get up. He had to move forward.

CHAPTER 5

Kevin's second period teacher had been saying something, he knew that much. He had heard her voice—the soft, monotonous voice he thought could be an effective antidote to insomnia—but he heard it without distinction, much the same we hear the sound of falling raindrops.

"Mr. Stottlemyer?" she asked, peering at him above her half-moon glasses. "Any thoughts?"

"Um, uh," he started, glancing helplessly to the students around him, who were miserably failing at suppressing giggles at his getting caught dozing. Last year, or any prior year, for that matter, he'd have felt embarrassed. Now, as he watched his father wage war with impending death, he found he didn't much care about such a petty matter.

"Sorry, ma'am."

She smiled softly. "Thinking about that St. Andrew's game, I suppose?"

Indeed. He had been thinking about that St. Andrew's game. Thanks for the reminder. Kevin had dominated the Lions last year: 22 points, 8 assists, 0 turnovers. He had been decent his freshman and sophomore years, playing here and there in spots on the varsity team. His role mostly consisted of giving the starter a quick breather, filling in at the end of the first and third quarters. Last year's game had been his first start, and nearly 2,000 people were there to see it. In 32 minutes of basketball he had become one of the most popular kids in school.

This was a basketball town. So, yes, Kevin had been thinking about basketball.

"I'd be lying if I said I wasn't, ma'am."

"I appreciate your candor, Mr. Stottlemyer, but if you could, I'd like you to turn your focus to my classroom, at least while you're in it. You can't change last night's game. It's over. Seeing as it's over, I'd like your mind to be with us."

"Yes ma'am."

Lyla Storm was no idiot: She knew boys didn't care much for girls' basketball. So she knew exactly what each one of the dozen or so boys were getting at when they dropped by her locker between classes to tell her good game, or that her ball dribbling was excellent, or that she should go out with them after a game sometime. The variations in the attempts were endless. None of them realized when they tried to talk basketball with Lyla Storm, they invariably came out looking dumber. Ball dribbling? Seriously? That's what you're going for? They think they're smooth. Aren't boys at least supposed to know the ability to dribble a basketball was called ball handling? Idiots. Idiots with big muscles and pretty smiles, sure. But still idiots. All of them.

She didn't say this, of course. No, she had become rather enamored seeing the stands packed to the brim to watch her play. Best not to alienate any member of her rapidly swelling fan base.

"You should come to as many as you can while I'm still here, because I'm going big time, you know," she would promise. "If you come, I'll be sure to put on a show for you. I always do."

Then she would saunter off to class, making sure to wiggle her butt just so. She never looked back, yet she knew they would be sneaking glances as she walked.

On this particular day, a crowd of three boys had approached Lyla between classes. They had been at the game last night. They watched her play, as they did for pretty much every home game, even though none of them had ever played basketball before. Their names were Matt, Lonnie and Danny. Lyla knew this, though she never actually acknowledged them by name, in case that might hint she gave a shit what they thought. Names meant you actually knew them. She didn't care to know them.

"She is perrrrrrfect," Danny crooned as Lyla walked by them to her class, just within earshot.

"Too dumb, bro," Matt countered. "Girl's a box of rocks. Hot, though. Definitely hot. Definitely fun to watch run around, mmhmm."

"For sure," Lonnie said. "Bet the only reason she gets into college is because she's so good at hoops."

They snickered and walked to their respective classes, just as Lyla was nearing hers. They couldn't have known she could hear them, the idiots three, as they'd now be known. Silently, she seethed.

Lyla knocked on the wooden door to Coach Koontz's office, where she was preparing her lesson plan for the next day's gym classes.

Koontz opened the door and gave her a wide smile. She was still in her sweatpants from that morning, when she had ushered Kevin and Lyla off the court, as she did every morning of the season. It must be nice to be a gym teacher. No dresses, no makeup, no 9-5 office job. Just sports and sweats.

"When are you going to learn to stop knocking and just walk in?"

"Some teachers find me rude, remember?" Lyla said in a mock peppy cheerleader voice, throwing her hands on her hips. Coach Koontz rolled her eyes.

"Can't imagine why."

"So," Lyla said, collapsing into the office chair Coach Koontz had been sitting on, kicking her feet up onto the desk, "whatcha got for me to do today?"

Coach Koontz picked up a stack of papers from a pile and dropped it in front of Lyla with a thud.

"Today's quizzes. The answer key is on top. Grade as many as you can before two-thirty and then I want you thinking about nothing but basketball, K?"

Lyla couldn't help but hide her disappointment. She had scored more than 40 points on just 15 shots last night. The girls team had won by, like, a billion. It was never even close. Yet she couldn't get a single compliment from her coach?

"Fine," she said, swiping the stack from her desk.

"Good," Coach Koontz responded, not looking up at the pouting Lyla. "I'll be in here if you need me."

Lyla stormed off to the empty gym, slamming the door behind her. Koontz glanced up, sighed, and shook her head.

"That girl," she muttered, then returned to her lesson plan.

Lyla didn't hear the bell ring. She had been lost in thought, sprawled out on the wooden gym floor, enjoying the lovely scents of wood and salt and leather. Yankee Candle should make this scent, she thought as she absentmindedly flipped through the stack of papers in front of her. There were words scrawled on them. She knew that. Yet she couldn't recall a single one she read.

Her mind had wandered. College applications. Basketball. Coach Koontz. Her parents.

Lyla was a senior now, a time that should be considered one of the best years of her life. All she felt was stress.

LSU had called her. They wanted her to play for them, to be a Tiger, to be the face of a budding program. She would be the girl who could lead them to a national championship.

"Sign with us," they had gently implored her, "or at least give us a verbal commitment. We don't want to recruit another guard, but if you don't, we'll have to explore our options."

So did UConn, the powerhouse for the past several years, winners of five national championships in a decade. She would continue that string of greatness, the coach had said. But they, too, needed her to commit.

Others phoned, emailed, wrote letters, visited. Tennessee came by for an in-house visit, and Lyla's mother, Sue, had made a fine dinner of steak and grilled asparagus in an effort to impress her. It tasted strangely wonderful to Lyla. She couldn't recall the last time her mother made her lunch, let alone cook dinner for her. That was left to her father, Mike. He packed everything, watched her diet. Turkey wasn't put on a sandwich, rather rolled up. Cutting out bread reduced the carbs. Her dessert was fat-free Jello and a cup of yogurt. Snack was carrots with light ranch. Her stomach growled at the thought.

The gym doors burst open and a handful of freckly kids sprinted in. Each of them held newspapers. She glanced up from the mass of papers. She had only graded three in an hour. Coach Koontz would be furious.

"Lyla!" they cried, all at once. There was probably 12 of them. From the looks of their baby faces and awkward haircuts, she guessed they were freshmen.

"Mmm?"

"The paper named you Player of the Week! Again! Congrats! Can you sign mine?" they clamored.

All of a sudden, there were newspapers in front of her, each kid shoving it in her face. She grabbed one and glanced at it.

The headline read: "The perfect Storm: Prep star named Player of the Week a record 20 times."

She allowed a smile.

"Well why wouldn't I sign your paper?"

She quickly summoned a beatific grin.

One handed her a red pen and Lyla scrawled her name in a practiced signature, loopy yet sharp, distinct and flashy, with a heart next to each one with her number 3 inside.

"Thanks, Lyla!" exclaimed a cheeky kid, who introduced himself as Harold, his red hair making his flushed cheeks seem impossibly rosy. "I'm gonna save this for when you go pro!"

"Just so long as you don't sell it," Lyla said, smiling her heart-melting smile. "Only so many people get a Lyla Storm signature in high school." She winked at him. He looked like he might faint. One by one, she signed the rest, leaving each kid with a

Lyla Storm signature and a wink. She sighed. It was kind of exhausting.

As the last one left, Coach Koontz swaggered into the gym, her long legs eating up huge swaths of court.

"Get those quizzes done for me?"

Oh. Right.

"Sorry, coach," she said, avoiding eye contact, handing her the unimpressive stack of three graded papers. "I, uh, got distracted."

Normally this would be the part where Koontz lit into her. Nobody was harder on Lyla Storm, with the exception of her father, than Coach Koontz. She had suspended her from the team for two weeks when Lyla was a sophomore. Lyla had scored a nifty, knifing layup in a game against Good Counsel, but the ref thought she saw a travel and whistled accordingly. Lyla responded in kind by flipping her the bird. Koontz responded in kind by putting her petulant butt on the bench.

As a junior, Lyla was well on her way to a career-high night, having put up 38 points in three quarters against an out of conference team, John Paul II. Coach Koontz benched her, not wanting to run up the score. Lyla punted a chair. Coach Koontz made her run suicides immediately after the game, directly in front of the John Paul II players while they waited for the bus. She ran until she puked.

Today, however, Coach Koontz was evidently feeling a bit magnanimous.

"It's alright, Storm," she said, scooping the stack of exams out of Lyla's arms. "Here, I have your report card."

Lyla's heart was ablaze with nerves at the sight of the manila envelope. She bit her lip and fidgeted. She could play basketball in front of a sold-out crowd but dammit did grades turn her stomach into an Olympic gymnast, flipping and tumbling and plummeting and crashing.

"Can you open it for me?"

Koontz smiled. It was sort of endearing, seeing Lyla so vulnerable.

"Sure."

She ripped open the envelope and scanned the white paper inside.

"Well," she began, pausing dramatically, grinning at Lyla's squeamish pacing. "Straight A's, again. As if there would be anything else."

Lyla slumped back onto the court. *What a relief.*

"I saw your fan club run in here a second ago, by the way," Koontz added, dropping Lyla's flawless report card on top of her. "Must be tough being the most famous person in Gaithersburg."

Lyla snorted. Tough? This is exactly what she wanted, wasn't it? Ever since she was little and her dad put a basketball in her hands, she dreamed of signing autographs, of being coveted, being loved, having her smiling face on the cover of the newspaper.

"You're going to be great one day," he had told her. She could remember it as if it were yesterday.

"Yes I am, Daddy."

And great she became.

But she couldn't help but wonder, sitting there on that gym floor, the same one that earned her all the fame and prestige and popularity every high schooler dreams of, if greatness was still everything she wanted.

CHAPTER 6

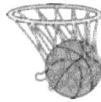

Bill Stottlemyer had made this drive before. Forty-five minutes of twisting backroads. Sweet and serene. No traffic or red lights or honking or even the purr of another engine.

It was only November, but the temperature was a biting 25 degrees. He still rolled the window down. When you're blessed with the knowledge that your days are numbered, you learn to soak up every last thing you once loathed: shoveling the driveway, the numb feeling your nose gets when a cold wind sweeps through, breathing in frosty air so deep your lungs burn with an icy chill, the smell of manure in the fields. Life is a beautiful thing. It's a shame it takes death to see it that way.

His Ford Explorer wound through the trees and he absorbed every last subtle curve. He figured on never making this trip again.

His body had been fighting brain cancer for several years, all but one of which had been unbeknownst to him. He had consciously been fighting it for less than a year, after the stroke led to his diagnosis. The doctors told him his time was running low. He underwent surgery and it had been somewhat successful but it was a delay more than anything, a purchasing of time in a life that was running out of it.

As he often did on these trips to the oncologist, he played the film of his life in his mind. His first thought went to his wife, that beautiful angel he had met when he was a scrub in Miami. He could remember the first time they met. She didn't even realize it. An assistant at nearby Florida Gulf Coast, she was in the stands. Bill couldn't help but notice that curvy blonde in the stands, hair pulled back in a tight ponytail. He asked a stadium staffer to introduce him to her after the game. Gulf Coast played the next night, she told him, and he didn't have to think twice. The next night he was the one in the stands, watching as she spent the next three hours screaming, all veins and blood pressure, blonde hair cascading wildly down her back. Oh, yes. That's the one. Six months later, he put a ring on her finger.

Two years after that they had their first of three, Kevin. Two more followed. A house. A fence. A dog. The American Dream. They were living it.

When Kevin turned 16, though, is when Bill's little memory film gets blurry. He began misremembering things, events, day-to-day duties, directions to places he had been 1,000 times before. Deep down, he knew something was amiss. He just couldn't face it. He was a hypocrite, playing the role of hero for his kids, imploring them to never back down to anyone, to shoot for the stars and every other dad cliché in the book. He couldn't even face his own opponent. Then came the stroke. If he wasn't going to acknowledge life, well, life was going to acknowledge him, in the office, of all places, just a few days before the state championship. His left arm had begun to tingle. He shook it, though it did nothing to alleviate the feeling. Then his vision smeared. He could hear his heart in his ears, feel it hammering his temples, drumming his wrists and neck. His face grew hot. He opened the door to the office—and then there was nothing. He blacked out, opening his eyes in a hospital, IVs running through both of his arms.

Tests ensued; he lost count of how many. Details seem insignificant when a doctor says "brain cancer" and "stroke" within 10 words of each other. It's amazing how many words we can say in a day, a month, a year, and how three can bring your entire world crashing down. He took it as he did anything else—just another opponent to beat. His children and wife cried. It was unfair, they said.

Yet it was perfectly fair. Life had been trying to warn him. Really, it had, but Bill had ignored it. Now he was in a hospital bed and quite fairly so. Try as his kids might to convince him otherwise, Bill was human and his mortality had suddenly gotten very, very real.

"Life," he told them at dinner one day, determined to keep his eyes dry and voice strong, "is the fairest thing we have in this world, because it is equally unfair to all of us. It holds no biases. We all have the same twenty-four hours each day, the same seven days each week, the same three hundred and sixty-five days each year. Good things and bad things happen every day. Today, a bad thing happened. Now it's up to me to decide how I deal with it.

"I have told you all, at some point, that life is ten percent what happens to you and ninety percent how you respond to it. It is now my time to live up to that standard."

The severity of the situation was kept from his children, even to this very day, as Bill was navigating the backroads to the hospital that had been his home away from home. Only Carla knew how serious this trip was, though Kevin was too old not to have at least an inkling. And bless her heart she had reacted with a long kiss and a hug and a "whatever you need, I'll be here, and I'll love you forever."

Bill Stottlemyer was going to die.

He was driving to the hospital to learn just how many days he had left on this Earth, how many shots he could see Kevin take, how many books little Jocelyn could read, how much energy Tim could inject into his life.

He made the final left turn into the hospital and parked the Explorer. He had left all of his medication at home. His doctors might frown but what could they really say? A frown was all they could realistically offer before a reassuring hand and whatever else may make his life—what was left of it—any easier.

The sliding doors whirred open and there was Dr. Brinkman, her normally 1,000-watt smile a little less charged but present nonetheless.

"Bill, how are we feeling today?"

He smiled and looked outside.

"I'm alive, aren't I? Blessed as I'll ever be."

She smiled and wrapped him in a warm hug. Doctors weren't supposed to get too close to their patients but Dr. Brinkman wasn't most doctors and Bill wasn't most patients.

It was a rare occasion when someone called him Bill. He was known as Coach. That was it. Just Coach. Anybody who said 'Coach' within a two-hour radius knew exactly who was being referenced. The Coach at Covenant Prep was both a coveted and fear-inducing position. Success meant a beloved status in the community. Failure meant quite the opposite.

In ten years as Covenant's coach, Bill had won six league titles and lost just 25 games. He couldn't recall the last time he ate at Greenmount Station, the town's local watering hole Gaithersburg denizens frequented after basketball games, and picked up his own tab, which is why he rarely ate there. Bill knew that most in Gaithersburg were not the richest folk. They should be spending money on their own family's meals.

Dr. Brinkman was different from most in Gaithersburg in that she did not care for sports. She cared for her patients and her patients only. This is exactly why Bill selected her as his oncologist. He would receive no special treatment.

The familiar scents of sick patients and latex filled Bill's nostrils as he followed Dr. Brinkman to his usual room. He would not miss those smells.

Dr. Brinkman closed the door shut behind her with a small "click," and when she turned, Bill noticed tears welling on the outside of her chocolate eyes.

"I don't know what to tell you," she said softly. She stared at her clipboard and her shoulders shuddered a bit. Bill could tell she was holding back sobs.

"Just a number, doc," Bill whispered. He didn't mean for his voice to have such a dramatic effect. That was just how his voice was these days, nothing more than a whisper. "Just a number."

"Ten at the most."

Bill took a deep breath, as big of an inhale as his lungs could handle, and let is out as slowly as he could. She did not mean years or months. She meant days. Ten days. The whirring machines beside his bed had been ineffective for some time. He knew this just as he knew his time alive was mortally limited. Ten days still hit him in the gut like a left hook.

"I'm so sorry, Bill."

The sobs commenced. He reached out and took her into his arms, her tears soaking the collar of his shirt, and soon they were a heaving, weeping mess. Dr. Brinkman could see him like this. Bill had long since decided that the only person who could see him weak and vulnerable would be Dr. Brinkman. At home, he would put up a façade of a strong man, healthy and full. Invincible. This was made difficult when Kevin or Tim or Jocelyn visited him in his room, when he was hooked up to the machines but he tried nonetheless. Here, at this small doctor's office outside of Gaithersburg, he would willingly show the man that cancer had reduced him to: delicate, mortal, beatable. He wasn't Coach to cancer. No, he was just another man, a very mortal, vulnerable man.

"I'm so sorry, I'm so sorry, I'm so sorry."

"It's alright, doc. I knew it wouldn't be long. Thank you for everything."

Bill didn't know what else to say. Prolonging the goodbye would only make things worse. She had more patients to treat. She couldn't focus on a dead man walking. He gripped her shoulder and looked her straight in the eyes, no different than how he used to look at his players.

"Be as good to your other patients as you were to me."

He wiped his eyes, took a deep breath and handed her a box of tissues that had been resting fortuitously on a nearby table. It was time to be strong again.

Then he walked out and hopped back into the Explorer, 45 minutes of winding roads away from telling his wife she would be a widow, from telling his children they would be fatherless.

CHAPTER 7

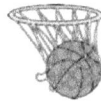

How do you tell three children that their father, their best friend, their role model, is going to be snatched away from them? That the jaws of death were just too strong to escape this time? That he'd be gone within 10 days and it could be any of the next 10? That they could go to school, play a basketball game, read a book, and walk in the house, and their father is gone?

How do you tell them that?

Bill had not been nervous in a very long time. Even when he played professional basketball, his nerves had been wrought of steel.

He had played in so many games that his body was trained to quell the butterflies. He didn't have time to get nervous when he was informed of his diagnosis. He had been unconscious for the trip to the hospital, much of the testing, and was still groggy, confused and dazed when Dr. Brinkman hit him with it.

Right now, though, Bill was nervous. He wanted to throw up. He sat at the kitchen table, pretending to read the newspaper, glazed eyes skimming latest opus *The Gazette* had written on Lyla Storm. The girl could play. If only she'd humble herself a bit.

The door swung open and tiny feet pitter-pattered against the wood floor. Tim.

"Daddy!" he squeaked, leaping onto Bill's lap. "Are you reading? Whatcha reading? Can I read with you? I don't know if I want to read. I read a lot at school. I don't really like what we're reading but I like to read."

Bill smiled and the dam broke. Almost a year's worth of pent up tears began pouring out. He hugged Tim as tightly as he could without breaking his tiny frame in two.

"Daddy," he said, his voice muffled through Bill's red shirt. "Your eyes are leaking."

"I'm sorry, buddy," he said as coherently as he could. "I just love you so much. I hope you know that."

"I love you too, Daddy. Why are you crying?"

"You'll know soon enough, buddy. Go put your stuff down and watch some TV. I think Modern Family is on."

"OK."

He pitter-pattered off, shooting a sidelong glance at his dad as he zipped into the living room.

Jocelyn would be next. Get it together. He took a long, shuddered breath and decided not to get it together at all. He went upstairs, waiting until everybody returned home. He would inform them all at once.

From his bed, he could hear Kevin and Jocelyn ask where Dad was. Carla told them he was resting, he'd be down for dinner then she lightly trod upstairs, where she knew he was not sleeping or resting, rather preparing.

"Ten days, huh?" she said, lightly shutting the door. She was wearing a purple long sleeved t-shirt and jeans. Her blonde hair spilled down her shoulders, which were still broad from her days as an athlete.

Bill nodded. God, his wife was so beautiful.

"I loved you since the day I saw you screaming at that girl for running the wrong cut, you know that?" he said, and he began to laugh.

"Jordan."

Carla laughed through pursed lips, still mad at that one wrong cut from that one player two decades ago. Bill loved that. A voracious competitor, his wife.

"She always did. Never ran it all the way through. Always cut it short and popped out for the three. I think she tried it a hundred times and never made one. Golly she drove me crazy. Almost as crazy as you."

"I knew right then and there I was in trouble."

"You big liar."

"It's true."

"Sure it is, baby."

She slipped into bed and delicately placed her head on his chest, allowing herself to melt into him. He reached a thick arm around her and slowly ran his big hands through her hair. She closed her eyes and Bill could feel tears beginning to spill down and puddle onto his shirt. It had absorbed far too many tears for a day.

"I'm not ready, Bill," she whispered. "Our kids don't need this. Not yet. Not when Joc is nine and Tim is eight. They have so much to look forward to with you. You have yet to scream at Tim for breaking curfew. Somebody has to get Kevin in line when he starts drinking like a college kid. You have yet to walk Jocelyn down the aisle. You can't leave. Not yet. You need to be here for those things we both know I can't do."

"I ain't dead yet, babe. I'll cram a life's worth of memories like only this big bear can and shoot, you're gonna raise 'em better than I ever could. You know it, too. They're smart like you, all of 'em."

"Oh, hush."

He hugged her tight, tight as he'd ever hugged her, though the effort sent a wave of wheezes and coughs exploding through his lungs. It was worth it. Absolutely, definitely, totally worth it.

For a few minutes, they lay there in silence until they could both smell the bacon-wrapped chicken from the oven. Dinner was ready. It was time.

"Ready?" she asked, kissing him gently on the cheek.

"Not a chance in the world."

"That's the thing about God, baby. He doesn't really wait until we're ready, does he?"

CHAPTER 8

This was not how Bill would have preferred it. This should have come maybe 20 years later, when he was grayer, wiser, when Jocelyn was a woman. But Bill did not have 20 years. He did not have 20 days. Hell, for all he knew, he didn't have 20 hours.

So there he was, head devoid of the dark brown hair he had evidently passed down to Kevin, 6-foot-4 frame emaciated and shrunken a bit yet still visibly muscular despite the cancer, standing at the beginning of the aisle at St. Mark's Lutheran Church. He was waiting for his 9-year-old daughter.

He had gotten the idea the day he'd lain in bed with Carla, just before he told the kids just how little time they had left with him. How do you pack a life's worth of memories in 10 days or less? He didn't know, but dammit if he wasn't going to try. What were the big events? What could he cover? For a girl, for Jocelyn, it was obvious. Jocelyn was going to get married one day, tough as it may have been for Bill to acknowledge at the time. She was only nine. Regardless, Bill was not going to leave this world without walking his baby girl down the aisle. No way.

She was the most beautiful thing he'd ever seen: white veil over her cherubic face, miniature dress blanketing her miniature body, tiny, white shoes on her feet. And her Lion King backpack strapped across her shoulders. This was Jocelyn's wedding day.

"Hi, baby girl," he whispered. Hot tears welled in his eyes. For the first time since he could recall, he didn't much care if she saw him cry.

"Hi, Daddy," she said in a soft voice. She was beaming. Her green eyes matched her mother's, just as her loving demeanor did. Bill always knew his little girl would turn out to be just like Carla, and there was little that made him happier than the thought of another Carla in the world.

He took her left hand with his right, and together, they walked down the aisle.

Jocelyn was too young to understand that Daddy would be gone soon. That it would just be Mommy and Timmy and Kevin—that her older brother would be the man of the house. She lived in an enviable world where there was still a Tooth Fairy and Santa Claus. This was not yet a reality she would be able to grasp.

At the end of the aisle, Kevin and Timmy waited. Kevin, in a smart, smoke gray suit, stared intensely at his shoes, painfully aware of what was happening. Timmy fidgeted in his jacket that was a few sizes too big, blissfully unaware of the gravity of the situation, though bright enough to understand something wasn't quite right. Carla did her best to keep her tears blotting on her turquoise dress. Jocelyn had picked it out when they went shopping the previous day for "bridesmaid" dresses.

Bill got down on one knee and faced his daughter, flipping over the veil so her light brown hair slipped down her shoulders and he could see right into those eyes that so wonderfully resembled her mother's.

"Joc, I want you to know that no matter what happens, I'm always going to be with you."

The walk had exhausted him. His voice was extra wheezy now.

"Right here, in your heart, that's where I'll be. One day, you'll understand all of this. For now, just know I love you so very much."

He hugged her and she hugged him back, as tight as a 9-year-old girl can hug a man. He didn't know what else to say. What can you possibly tell your daughter when you are about to die? He kissed her on the cheek, then the forehead, the other cheek. He put his head on hers, so his tears melted onto her cheeks. One last hug. He rose, and Kevin scooped her up in his arms. She was crying, though she had no idea why.

That day was a Sunday, and it was for memories. Bill wasn't sure how memories worked in Heaven. He hoped he'd be able to take them with him. Yet they were not for him. They were for Jocelyn, who he hoped would recall, when she was walking down the aisle for her real wedding, her father had indeed given her away, and that she did not walk down the aisle alone. They were for Timmy. After the mini-ceremony at St. Marks, Bill took Timmy to the arcade, where they played pinball and hammered gophers. Bill teased Timmy about girls. Timmy begged him to stop. They both laughed and laughed until their stomachs hurt and they eased the pain with ice cream.

They were for Kevin. Three hours at the arcade left Timmy exhausted and giggling more out of delirium than anything. Bill returned him, ice cream still smeared on his cheeks, to Carla at their house. He motioned for Kevin to hop in.

Kevin hadn't taken the news well. He was the only child in the Stottlemyer household old enough to really understand it. This did not to make it any more bearable. Kevin and his father had one of those relationships other children and parents envy and try to emulate though inevitably fail. Theirs was a relationship that could not be replicated. Nothing about Kevin and Bill was forced. Just a natural genetic code, a gift from God above. He played basketball like Bill. He ate like Bill. He walked like Bill. When people called the house phone, they confused Kevin's voice for Bill's, and he took that as a wonderful compliment.

"You're going to be just like him," they said. Kevin would smile from ear-to-ear.

Kevin had said nothing the night before, when Bill informed his children he had but days remaining with them. He had said nothing the entire day, either. Bill could tell Kevin had been crying, from the puffy red rims around his eyes. But that was it. Kevin was a closed book, just like his father.

Bill's son slipped quietly into the passenger seat and pressed his nose against the frosted window. Bill began to drive.

Kevin knew exactly where they were going as soon as they made a right at the end of their street.

"Dad." He smushed his face deeper into the window, as if he could melt right through it. "Don't."

Bill said nothing.

Kevin groaned and sank into his seat, as if the weight of the world was somehow lighter the deeper he buried himself into the passenger seat of an SUV. It wasn't.

As Bill had prearranged, the lights were on in Stottlemyer Arena, though nobody was there. Two basketballs awaited at midcourt. He picked one up for himself and tossed the other to Kevin.

"You know," he began, not addressing Kevin directly, looking instead at the hoop. "I used to be pretty good at this game.

Couldn't be stopped in high school. Scored sixty-five in a game once. Couldn't miss."

He took a 3-pointer and it sank through with a swish and an echo of the ball bouncing away.

"In college, as you know, I was a four-year All-American. Real cocky. Thought I was God's gift to hoops even though I stood barely taller than you do now."

Another shot. Another swish.

"Then the pros came and I was humbled. I was too small, too slow. Teams kept me around because I was a good teammate and could still shoot lights out but I knew I'd never make it in the pros. Too slow to get my shot off. Even still, I couldn't bear to give it up. I never thought I'd love anything in the world as much as playing basketball.

"And then you came around."

Bill finally turned to look at Kevin, who hadn't moved from midcourt, studying his basketball with a profound intensity.

"And when I watched you play, I thought it was the greatest thing that has ever happened. Nothing made me happier than watching you score a bucket. Remember the first one you scored? Against the orange team in Gaithersburg Rec?"

The corners of Kevin's mouth twitched. He nodded.

"Luckiest thing I've ever seen. You baseball-threw it from thirty feet. No idea why you thought that was a good idea. Banked that sucker in. Thought it would break the backboard you chucked that thing so hard. Not sure if I've ever laughed so hard since."

"Yea, well, I remembered watching you on TV," Kevin said, slowly. His voice sounded strange to him after not using it for nearly 24 hours. "You could make it from that far back without even trying. I wanted to impress you."

"Oh, you impressed me alright. You fell in love right then and there. Basketball was it. We tried to get you into baseball, football, soccer, track and you were having none of it. All you wanted to do was play ball."

"Because I wanted to be like you."

"Which is why I brought you here, Kev."

Kevin looked in his father's eyes for the first time since the talk the night before.

"I know what you've been going through. I know this is our place, where we grew close. Most fathers have some corny father-son bonding bullshit at some sleep-away camp or church retreat or something. We had hoops. I know that's why you played awful the other night."

Kevin raised an eyebrow.

"Oh, yes, I watched the film. Had Coach Snyder bring it to the house the next day. You can't be scared of this court, this ball, this sport, Kevin. You're better than that, son. The moment you let fear get to you is the moment you lose everything, you hear? Trust me, I know. Think I handled this cancer business with all guts and courage? No, sir. I was scared out of my mind. But I wasn't scared for me. Heavens no. I was scared to lose you, to lose Joc and Timmy and your mother. I should have swallowed that fear, Kev. It's what you need to do right now or you're going to regret it for the rest of your life, and, gosh, you have so much of it in front of you."

He shot again. Another swish.

"This game will not remind you of me hooked up to machines, or forgetting plays, or anything to do with me being sick. Only if you let it. Don't let it. No, this game will remind you of when we would come here at six in the morning and shoot so long we'd forget lunch. It will remind you of when we made it to a state championship. It will remind you of when the ball was almost bigger than you and you chucked in a thirty-footer."

Kevin shook his head. He dropped the ball.

"Kevin, I cannot make you do anything anymore. Your life is yours and yours only, but I want you to keep playing this game. I want this to be the piece of me you carry on. You can take down every photograph or little keepsake you have of me but I want you to keep playing basketball."

Kevin watched the ball roll over the court. He closed his eyes and took a deep breath. He had always wanted to be like his father. He just didn't expect he'd need to become him so soon.

"Can we have the guys over for dinner?"

Bill smiled. Tears began welling in his eyes. His son was growing up.

"Wouldn't have it any other way."

"Let's go. It's cold in here."

CHAPTER 9

Jared snorted at the text. He hadn't seen the name "Kevbo" pop up on his phone in some time.

"Team dinner at my house at 5:30. Mom made spaghetti and rolls and whatnot."

Then he read the last line: "Coach wants you there."

He swallowed hard, read it again: "Coach wants you there." Jared hadn't talked to or seen Coach since before last year's championship game. He glanced at the half-drunk Budweiser in his hand and put it down, feeling suddenly and inexplicably ashamed. A good amount had changed since Coach abandoned them.

Why had he abandoned them? Coach never gave a reason for disappearing just days before the title game, simply sending a message to the team that he'd be out. He officially retired a few weeks after the season and the gym was named after him a few days later, skipped championship game or not. There must have been a good reason, right? Jared hadn't seen or heard from him since the game and he hadn't attempted to reach out.

So why now? Why did Coach want to see him and the rest of the Stags he deserted, now, fresh off a humiliating loss, when he wasn't even coaching anymore?

It was 4:45. Jared lived just a 15-minute walk away from Kevin's house, or a two-minute drive if his rusty old truck was feeling up to it. He swigged his Budweiser and burped. It had been awhile since he'd last eaten a home-cooked meal, which had come, not coincidentally, at the Stottlemyers.

Jared had never met his mother and his pops didn't know how to cook, not that he would have, anyway. Pops was more interested in beer than he was his own kids. Never went to a game. Never helped with homework. Jared wasn't even sure if Pops knew he played basketball or attended Covenant Prep. Steve had taken care of him best he could, but ole Steve-O, no saint himself, didn't know much about taking care of kids; didn't exactly have the best role models. So when Pops skipped town a few years back and it was just Steve-O and Jared, not a whole lot changed. Jared slept a little better, if anything, now that he didn't have to worry about getting the belt when Pops came back half-cocked on whiskey. The only thing that changed, for the most part, was that Jared went to Kevin's more often and Steve enlisted in the Air Force as soon as he got the chance.

Jared glanced at the jars of peanut butter and jelly that had served as lunch and dinner since Steve deployed four months ago. His stomach growled. Yeah, he could use a home-cooked meal. He crumpled the can of Budweiser and hurled it against the wall, spraying it an ugly shade of tan with beer.

Carla Stottlemyer was admittedly a bit nervous. She wasn't sure it was the best idea to have the boys over. The last time they had seen Coach, he had been strong as an ox, the town's hero. As boys' minds sometimes do, theirs invariably built up the image of Coach into something mythical in his absence, particularly with how poorly Coach Snyder was handling the team.

Nevertheless, one by one they piled in. Brandon Thompson, the nifty point guard, lit up when he saw Carla. He used to come over for sleepovers and dinners three or four times per week.

"Hey, Mama," he said as he walked through the door without knocking. That's what he called her: Mama. That was the role Carla filled with a good number of Kevin's teammates. The Stottlemyers were Gaithersburg basketball royalty and she was the first lady.

"Hey, sweetie." She hugged him tight. Tears began to well. Already? She was losing her natural southern grit. She blinked quickly. "Kevin's in the living room."

"Smells awesome in here, Mama."

He bounded off to the living room.

Next was Warren, the big man with the awful hands and the only black kid on the team and Nate, the deceptively athletic and little-used power forward with the big gut and soft hands. Then Garrett, Jordan, Bryan and Andy. By 5:15, the entire team was piled in the living room, save for Jared. Carla hadn't seen him in, gosh, how long had it been? Half a year?

Brandon had been close with Kevin but Jared and her son had been inseparable. When they were freshmen, they talked about college. They were going to room together and lead the Maryland Terrapins to a national title. Then they'd go pro, make millions and buy a house right next to Covenant Prep. They'd coach the team to a state title or 10. Carla never pried into Jared's home life but she knew the obvious red flags when she saw them. He slept at their house more often than his. She saw the way his eyes lit up when she made dinner, as if the boy had never seen a proper cooked meal before. He was unfailingly polite and gracious, which belied the wild stories she'd heard about him—the drinking, the drugs, the girls. Carla had called Jared's house dozens of times but the phone was never on. She'd driven by and knocked yet there was never an answer. It broke her heart when Kevin and Jared fought at practice on more than one occasion last year but boys will be boys. She grew up in a house of five of them. They'd get over it.

Carla loved all of the boys on the Prep team as if they were sons of her own. Their home had become, at one point or another, a second home to most of them. But no one face made her happier than seeing Jared's, five minutes late, on her doorstep.

He smiled a smile capable only of a boy who was fully aware of how handsome he was.

"Hey, Mrs. Stottlemyer," he said.

Jared wore a stained shirt and wrinkled tie that was tied too short, a good two inches above his bellybutton. The other boys wore mostly sweatpants and various other Prep basketball gear.

"It's so good to see you, sweetie."

They hugged and now Carla could no longer hold back the tears. Bill had been the only reliable father figure Jared had in his life, and though he hadn't been able to be present in Jared's life all that much these past few months, that was about to be permanently gone.

Jared looked at her, eyes wide with concern.

"Just go in the living room, honey. The spaghetti is on the table. The boys have already started."

He paused, unsure of how to react and slipped past her.

Carla had made eight boxes of spaghetti, topped with more than 100 meatballs. Servings per box were 10. A team of 12 boys ate every last noodle. Teenage boys. Insatiable pits, all.

They lazed on the couch, stuffed and happy, save for Kevin. He hadn't touched his food. Too nervous. Couldn't eat. Barely spoke. A college basketball game played in the background.

"I want to apologize," he said abruptly, to no one in particular, eyes finding a sauce-stained circle on their cream carpet. Probably Warren. Dude was clumsy as all get out. "I haven't been myself lately. Haven't been a good teammate."

He looked around at his team, of which he used to be considered the unquestioned leader.

"Haven't been a good friend."

His eyes found Jared's. Jared looked away and fumbled with his tie.

"I do not want to make excuses. I've been doing that for the last six to eight months. There is a reason and I'm sorry I've hidden it. I'm not even sure if it was my secret to hide but whatever. Probably should have told y'all anyway. Each one of you are family to me. Some I'd say are brothers. Others, like a cousin I really don't like but I'm obligated to hang out with here and there because we're family."

They laughed. It took even Kevin by surprise that he was able to muster some humor. It helped melt the pit of ice that had taken up residence in Kevin's stomach.

Bill listened from the kitchen, hands clasped in Carla's, her head on his chest. He buried his face in her hair, which smelled deeply of peaches. They swelled with pride as their boy became a man.

"My father coached all of us. I've been blessed to have him as my dad for this long."

Kevin paused. He gritted his teeth. This was the hard part.

"We won't have him for much longer."

His teammates remained silent, but the looks on their faces asked 1,000 questions. Best to dive straight into it.

"He didn't coach last year's championship game because he was in surgery. He had been coaching the entire year with brain cancer. He had probably been coaching years with brain cancer. I don't know. I don't really know how cancer works. I just know last year it got bad."

More looks. More unspoken questions.

"They found it too late. Can't be cured. His medicine stopped working a while ago. I don't know how long exactly. Doctors gave him ten days."

The silence was profound. It was as if God had simply taken all the air out of the room. Warren stopped rubbing his belly. Brandon slipped off the couch to the floor, holding his knees close to his chest like a child. Jared remained stoic, his hands frozen to his tie, eyes locked into a thousand-yard stare. Kevin could hear the ticking of the clock from the kitchen, the buzzing of a fly in the air, the electricity humming through the light bulbs, the soft creaking of a house under the weight of a high school basketball team.

"I'm sorry I didn't tell y'all sooner. I should have. I didn't know how to handle it. Now I do. I'm going to—we're going to keep playing basketball, and we're going to win. We're going to play like

Coach taught us to play. I'm going to be the friend you remember me being, the teammate you remember playing with, the basketball player that I like to think I am. We are going to win for Coach."

Silent tears were streaming down many of the players' faces. Around the corner, Bill and Carla embraced and strode into the room.

The boys looked up at their Coach, 30 pounds lighter than he was the last time they'd seen him. His skin was different, grayer. Yet he was still commanding.

"I'm sorry, boys," he said, and he tried damn hard to restore a little power in his voice. He wheezed instead. "I am. There is a better way to tell you than this. Should have told you long ago. For that, I apologize. I look around this room and I see twelve boys who have become young men. I see twelve sons. I'm proud to have been a part of your lives. I like to think I helped raise you, to become the excellent group of young men you have become. I like to think I will leave this Earth knowing I leave behind a group who will make it a better place. There is not much for me to say here, aside from I love you all. There are more important things to life than basketball. I want you to wake up every single day and better yourselves from the person you were yesterday. Make each day a good day. Either way, it's going to go on with or without you."

His lungs were grasping for air now. The past few days had been a flurry of activity, more than he'd had in months. His body was shutting down.

"It has taken me too long to realize that. Be strong, boys. You will never know how many people you are inspiring, only that it is more than you could imagine. I don't want you to be presented with a circumstance like mine to realize that."

Kevin stood and hugged Coach, which seemed to be a signal for the other players to do the same. One by one, they hugged Coach, told him they loved him. They hugged Carla, told her they loved her, too. Then they walked out the door. Until only Jared remained, still motionless on the couch. He hadn't spoken a word since Kevin first addressed the team.

"Coach," he whispered. "What am I supposed to do?"

Jared didn't know weakness. Ever. He loathed it. Vulnerability? That was for the weak. Yet there he sat, fumbling for words. Weak and most definitely vulnerable.

"I don't have a dad. My brother is gone. You're it. You're the reason I do my homework or at least some of it. You were the reason I still showed up to practice sober, mostly. That's gone. There is nobody left who would be disappointed in me. How am I supposed to live a life like that, you know? How am I supposed to live in a world with nobody who freakin' cares?"

Bill smiled. Because sometimes, in the strangest of moments, a smile is the only thing you can offer.

"There is always someone who cares, son." He put his hand on Jared's shoulder and gripped it tight. "You have my beautiful wife, who dotes on you enough that it should make me jealous. You have my son, who loves you like a brother whether he wants to admit it or not. And you have a team full of brothers who would put their life on the line for you, though I certainly hope it doesn't come to that. There is always, always, always someone who cares. Sometimes you just have to open your eyes and look."

Jared nodded and sniffed and hugged Coach so hard that Coach couldn't breathe for a moment.

"I love you."

Jared went to walk out the door but something compelled Kevin to grab his arm. Jared had been his best friend until all of a sudden he wasn't. They had done everything together as kids then something changed, in that abrupt way they can in high school. They began fighting at practice. Jared began drinking where Kevin set 5 a.m. alarms. Jared slept with basically every girl at Prep and a few elsewhere, too, and Kevin took Mandy on dates. Their paths had diverged, leaving basketball as the only string that held an increasingly fragile relationship together, until not even basketball could do it. Kevin figured it had hit a tipping point when he missed those free throws to lose last year's championship. He and Jared didn't speak for weeks then months, not a word really until this season loomed close.

"We're gonna get through this," Kevin said, looking his friend in the eyes. "We're gonna be OK."

Jared touched his forehead to Kevin's, squeezed his shoulder.

"You're my brother, man. I love you."

Kevin nodded and hugged his best friend and then Jared was gone.

Bill collapsed onto the couch. The effort of speaking and standing for so long had drained him. He glanced at Kevin.

"This is your team again. Now go take it."

CHAPTER 10

Kevin had longed for this feeling. He stood just to the left of center court, outside the circle where Warren was set most likely to lose another jump ball, this one to the hulking center from Good Counsel named Bruke, a 6-foot-10, 260-pound behemoth of a teenage boy. It was the most fitting name Kevin thought he had ever heard. To the right of Kevin was Jared, floppy hair already matted in sweat. Playing safety near Prep's basket was Brandon, the speedy point guard with the fast hands. Bryan, the 6-foot-3 small forward, stood opposite Kevin, awaiting a potential miracle tip from Warren.

Every Prep player had scrawled "COACH" in red marker onto the tongues of their blue shoes. It felt nice to play for someone other than themselves.

For the first time since the last time his father saw him play, the basketball court was Kevin's home, his sanctuary. His father was alas at peace, having given into the fight against cancer, and Kevin was, too. The funeral was long and well attended. More than 1,000 people showed up to offer their condolences. Most hadn't known about Coach's precarious state, only that he had abruptly given up coaching before the title game. The majority of the town was surprised the boys never once considered delaying the match up with Good Counsel, or just forfeiting it altogether. This was Coach, after all, a prominent figure not just in basketball, but in the very fabric of the community. His death was felt like an earthquake in Gaithersburg.

Good Counsel offered to push the game a week and Coach Snyder polled the boys to gather their opinions but they weren't having it.

Coach said to play, so play they would.

Kevin didn't grieve with the rest of Gaithersburg. He had quietly done it for the past year, on his own. It helped him, actually, fighting through the grieving process for a year rather than have the weight of it all dumped on him at once. He learned acceptance, responsibility. His family was now his, though family now had two meanings: the one in his house and the one on the court. He was the man of both.

The ref tossed the ball up in the air and Bruke predictably swatted it before Warren even thought about jumping and Brandon scrambled to where the Good Counsel point guard corralled it in.

"Twenty-two!" Kevin called out, waggling his index and middle fingers in the air, signaling that his Stags would be dropping into a trapping man-to-man defense. The idea was to force the ball into the corners, spring the trap and jump the passing lanes. Good Counsel relied on its big man because the guards were prone to turning it over. Trapping them, as the strategy went, should result in easy buckets going the other way.

Kevin found his voice was steady, icily confident, the way it had always been prior to this year. The boys clapped their hands twice and the home crowd did the same, roaring to life in a beautiful chorus.

The students had ordered specially made shirts for the rest of the season, red ones with "COACH" written in big white lettering on the front.

Not a single person sat.

Brandon angled his feet, cutting off the Good Counsel guard's path to the middle, forcing him to the right wing, closer to the trap. Bruke saddled up to Brandon's left, setting a pick that was designed to free up the middle of the court. Warren, tasked with guarding the enormous center, remained in the lane—there was no sense in chasing Bruke outside of it—clogging up the middle and preventing cutters from having an open lane. Kevin, though, whose man was lazily idling near the left corner, an obvious tell that this was a two-man set play for a pick and roll, saw the play unfolding and cheated up. The point guard crossed over, pushing towards Bruke, just as Kevin thought he might, and Kevin sprung forward.

He timed it perfectly. Just as the guard was rolling off Bruke's pick, Kevin was full speed, left hand outstretched exactly where the guard had turned the corner. He plucked the ball off his hands and smoothly converted it for a layup the other way.

The crowd crowed and stomped. Kevin banged his chest down the court, his court. It had his family's name scrawled in cursive on the very wood. He was going to own it. He was back. Prep was back.

Kevin couldn't be stopped. The touch he had developed over those countless morning practices returned, like an old friend who had moved away for a year. Electricity was pulsing through his veins. He hit four 3-pointers in the first five minutes. When the Good Counsel coach, a short, stubby man with a bald head and a leather jacket, called for a box-and-one on Kevin—a defense designed to stop one player—he carved them up with assists: drive and dish to Jared on the wing, drive and flip to Warren in the middle, cut and collapse the defense to leave Brandon or Bryan unguarded up top.

There was no way Good Counsel and its stubby coach could have prepared for the storm that hit them that dreary Tuesday night. Coach Snyder let his Prep boys have at it. Perhaps sensing the personal significance of the game, he left Kevin in for every minute. Jared, Brandon, Bryan and Warren were pulled after the third quarter, when the Stags were leading by 26 and finishing the game was merely a formality.

Kevin finished with 38 points, a career high. Jared netted 20 more and Brandon another 17 in a 92-56 Prep win. Kevin smiled and smiled, a beatific smile, and he cried a different kind of tear that night, one of happiness and, maybe, he thought, even relief. He could live his life again.

A reporter from *The Gazette* pulled him aside afterwards, asking him a series of questions Kevin wouldn't remember, followed by answers Kevin forgot immediately after they left his mouth. He only wanted to be with his team, his family, in the cauldron of joy that had become the locker room. The reporter freed him, thanking him for his time and expressing his sorrow about his father. Kevin hugged him. He didn't know why. He was happy. Who cared? Then he sprinted into the locker room, the smell of salt and sweat and socks and teenage boy filling his nose. Jared nearly tackled him.

"That's how you play, boy!" he roared.

Brandon slapped him on the butt. Bryan went for a hug but tripped and clung, laughing and giddy, to Kevin's jersey. Kevin returned the hug before stepping onto a metal chair, addressing his half-naked group of brothers.

"Prep is back, baby!" he bellowed, voice cracking just a touch, and the boys bellowed right back. Then his voice softened, as did his gaze. "I want to tell y'all," he said, eyes finding not the floor, as they had so often for the past year, rather as many of his teammates as possible, "how much y'all mean to me, how much y'all showing up to dinner meant. I know I haven't been myself for a while, and now hopefully y'all understand. Obviously losing my dad sucks, is gonna suck for a long, long time, but I've been doing my crying for too long. Too long. My family—we're happy he's no longer in pain. He's in a better place. And so are we."

He pointed to every teammate as he said this, finding every pair of eyes in the room.

"This season we're playing for my dad. And I tell you what, if we play like this, we're not losing another game."

The boys whooped and yelled as one. Kevin hopped off the chair and onto the tile floor to more hugs and butt-slapping.

Yes. Prep was back.

The girls team, of course, didn't need another source of inspiration to play well. By the time Kevin meandered out of the locker room an hour later, exhausted and emotionally spent, they were obliterating Good Counsel 65-16. It was only the third quarter.

Lyla had already scored 35 and Coach Koontz had replaced her with Tara, who was fumbling around in that endearingly reckless manner of hers.

Kevin collapsed into his incognito spot in the corner, where Timmy and Jocelyn were waiting with congratulations and hugs.

"A hero," Timmy called him.

"The best basketball player in the whole wide world," Jocelyn added.

Kevin grinned. His father had been right. He was always right. Everything was going to be just fine. Kevin looked skyward, at the wooden roof with the red banners hanging from it and well beyond and sighed a satisfying, exhausted sigh.

"Thanks, Pops," he whispered, throwing his arms around his siblings. "I love you."

Maryland Christian Athletic Conference Standings

Boys

St. Andrew's 2-0

Bishop O'Connell 2-0

Bishop McNamara 1-1

Good Counsel 1-1

Covenant Prep 1-1

Bishop Ireton 0-2

Gonzaga 0-2

St. Anselm's 0-2

Girls

Covenant Prep 2-0

Bishop O'Connell 2-0

Gonzaga 2-0

Good Counsel 1-1

St. Andrew's 1-1

St. Anselm's 1-1

Bishop Ireton 0-2

Bishop McNamara 0-2

CHAPTER 11

Prep was rolling. The boys won their next eight games. The girls, to the surprise of none, did the same. No team had come within 12 points of the boys, the closest being a former powerhouse in Bishop O'Connell and even then, the score indicated a closer game than it actually was. Prep had been winning by 25 at the end of the third quarter when Coach Snyder pulled the starters. As for the girls, well, Lyla had outscored all but one of their opponents by herself and she made sure everyone was aware of it.

School was a madhouse. Kevin couldn't walk anywhere between classes without being congratulated by teachers and students. Banners had become ubiquitous. Mandy was making a new batch of brownies for the boys seemingly every day. Bryan had somehow landed a good-looking date to the winter dance, a tall blonde by the name of Marisa.

"You know the world's coming to an end soon," Jared grumbled in the locker room before practice one day, "when Bryan snags the second-best date on the team."

The team thought it was uproarious. Bryan just took a bite from his Snickers bar and grinned, a chocolate-toothed grin.

"Basketball, bro," he mumbled through bites. "Gets me the ladies."

Jared had even curtailed his drinking. Whether that was because of Coach's passing or basketball, nobody could really say for sure, save for Jared, and Jared didn't talk much when he was sober.

Kevin, feeling a little bolder than usual—he was, after all, averaging 24 points per game during the win streak—got a tattoo, angel wings over his heart, with "Coach" inscribed in the halo above the wings. His mother had never been a big fan of someone etching something onto their skin that would remain there for the rest of their life but she cried when Kevin came home with it, and he was pretty sure they were happy tears.

Lyla, despite her setting and resetting the school single-game scoring records several times over, had even begun to ease back on her abrasive arrogance. Her and Kevin even spoke warmly—well, warmer—during their morning shoot-arounds, which got earlier and earlier with each passing win.

"Your shot isn't so ugly any more, you know," she said once, and Kevin thought it was the nicest thing she had ever said to him.

Neither team could lose. Wouldn't allow it. Not now. Not with the season being dedicated to Coach. Not with Kevin still playing for a scholarship offer and Lyla for every record in the Prep books. Losing just wasn't an option, plain and simple. *The Gazette* continued to roll out story after story on the team. Lyla lost count of the "Perfect STORM" headlines. Couldn't they think of a better play on words? As for the boys, it was inspirational, what was happening at Prep—going undefeated since the loss of a huge community figure, the father of possibly the best player on the team.

Even Coach Snyder had begun to gather some support throughout Gaithersburg. He was, as all coaches are in their beginning days, kept at arm's length by the Prep faithful. This had been done with Coach, too. They had to feel him out before accepting him as the full-time basketball coach, which, in the town of Gaithersburg, was more important than the mayor or police chief.

Greenmount Station named a burger after him during the win streak and that seemed to issue the final verdict: Coach Snyder was alright.

The team thought so, too. Coach Snyder had relinquished control of the locker room to Kevin, a cognizant move on his part. Jared staying sober, for the most part, didn't hurt either.

Everything was, well, it was perfect.

Then Friday rolled around. January 26th. No player, student, parent, teacher or coach at Prep will ever be able to forget that day.

That was the day the world crashed again.

It was a game day. The Stags were set to host lowly St. Anselm's, who was 2-8 and would need nothing shy of divine intervention to beat Prep, and at the time, divine intervention was something that was happening for Prep, not the other way around. In a rare show of panache, Coach Koontz announced that Tara would be starting over Lyla. If it had been anyone else, Lyla would have been livid. But this was Tara. Nobody could argue against putting in Tara, especially when the idea, shockingly enough, had originated from Lyla Storm herself. Tara was giddy. Throughout the entire school day, boys she had never met before gave her high fives. One bought her lunch and wished her luck.

As they always did on home games, Tara and Lyla walked home together, grabbing lunch at Snickerdoodles, a quaint coffee shop off Main Street. Tara was the monumentally superstitious type. She hadn't strayed from her order of three blueberry muffins and a caramel latte since the last time Prep lost a home game, which was never in the three-plus years Tara had been a member of the team. This also meant that Lyla, regrettably, couldn't order anything else but a plain bagel with honey butter. Lyla used to fight with Tara over it, but her friend was not one to budge on such serious matters as the karmic balance of the world, which ostensibly hung in a plain bagel and honey butter, so Lyla relented.

"Hello, ladies," the barista, a friendly man named Tony, said. "The usual, I presume?"

"Yes, Mr. Tony!" Tara squealed. She loved being recognized in town. Tony handed them their orders and wished them luck, to which Tara squealed again. It made her feel like a celebrity.

"So," Tara said between sips of her latte. "Have you narrowed your list down yet?"

The list. Everybody was talking about the list. Where was Lyla going to commit to play college? Reporters called at all hours of the day. Her father held her hostage in hours-long lectures over the importance of coaches, playing time, offenses and defensive systems. The only person who never really feigned any interest in the matter at all was Sue, Lyla's mother, which sort of irked the Prep star—didn't she care where she went to school?—but, at the same time was a wonderful relief, as it took one person off the manifest of people who needed to know where Lyla was going to school and needed to know rightthissecond. There were two people, aside from Lyla, who had any earthly clue where Lyla was going to go to college: Tara and Coach Koontz.

"I love love loveeeee LSU," Lyla said, nibbling on her bagel. "But Maryland—
oh, I just love that campus! And I've always been a Terps fan, you know? Which means Duke is out of the picture. No way. Ugh, disgusting. Could you imagine me playing for Duke? That Jack Miller kid, I mean, goodness gracious is he hot, but I still can't

believe he'd go there. Traitor. Syracuse is nice but, oh, the snow. There's so much snow."

As she said this, she glanced out the window, where flurries were beginning to dance from the gray sky above.

"I want to go someplace warm, I think."

"Yea, let's go someplace warm."

That was another element that nobody outside of the Tara-Lyla-Koontz triumvirate knew—Lyla and Tara were a package deal. When coaches offered Lyla a scholarship, she leveraged a manager position for Tara. If they didn't like it, oh well. That was her one and only condition.

"Ok then," Lyla said, grinning. "It's LSU or Florida State. What do you think?"

"Well, LSU has the better med school," Tara said. "It's top five in the country. I say LSU."

"Alright," Lyla shrugged. "Right now the order is LSU, Florida State and Maryland."

Life was that simple sometimes for Lyla Storm.

From Snickerdoodles, it was a quarter mile walk to Lyla's house. Tara practically skipped. Lyla laughed and smiled. She hadn't seen her friend this excited in her entire life. Except perhaps when Tara, who had never received a 'B' in her life, won a debate contest. But no, not even then.

They were at the corner of Main Street and Hartwick Drive when Lyla heard it. Tara had been gabbing about winter dance, how maybe if she scored enough points in that night's game a popular boy might take notice and ask her. She hadn't heard the screeching wheels that Lyla had. Lyla froze where she was. She couldn't see the source from around the corner, where trees blocked her view. It was then she realized the drivers would not be able to see Tara, who had not heard the cars. She was skipping across the road. Tara, lost in a world of imagined basketball glory and hot winter dance dates, hadn't been paying attention. The light had turned green. She shouldn't have crossed. A silver Chevy peeled around the corner first, going at least 75, by Lyla's judgement. A red one tailed right behind it. The speed limit was 35 and the light snow had begun to coat the ground in a filmy white layer. Lyla could barely make out the blur of the gold, cross-shaped Chevy logo before the car careened around the corner on the inside. Street racers. That's what they called themselves. Really, they were just a bunch of high school punks in shitty, supped up cars who were dumb enough to find pleasure in the thrill of imminent death from moronic driving. Tara heard the peels as both cars straightened up from drifting around the bend. She stiffened in an awkward mid-skip posture, terrified, eyes wide as saucers. She didn't have a second to react.

The silver Chevy veered to the left but it was too late. The tires squealed in an attempt to gain traction but the snow wouldn't allow it. It hurtled straight into Tara and she went flying backwards, a human cannonball.

Chaos.

Lyla screamed and dropped to her knees. Her vision instantly blurred with tears. *What do I do, what do I do, what do I do?*

She could barely make out the shapes of the silver and red Chevys bolting into the distance, around another bend. She brought her hands to either side of her face, attempting to block out everything around her. Her cheeks grew hot. She sobbed into the sidewalk. Her friend had just been hit by a car. She yanked her face off the cement and looked around frantically. People were running everywhere, some screaming into telephones, others screaming into nothingness, like Lyla.

Where had Tara gone?

She wished she hadn't looked. Tara lay in a crumpled heap, a good 35 feet from where Lyla now stood. Her legs and arms were twisted in ways Lyla knew they shouldn't. She knew instantly that virtually every bone in Tara's body was broken. She attempted to move but couldn't. Her legs had turned to stone. Lyla was paralyzed, by what exactly? Fear? Shock? She didn't know. She simply couldn't move. Dozens had come to Tara's aid, kneeling down beside her. Sirens wailed somewhere in the distance. Lyla collapsed again, curling up onto the cold, hard cement, and sobbed and sobbed until the world went black and cold and she could no longer feel a thing.

Lyla wasn't sure if she lost consciousness or just cried herself to sleep right there on that sidewalk, but when she next opened her eyes, she was in a room she had never seen before. From where she lay on an uncomfortably stiff bed, she noted the robins-egg blue walls and the two chairs near the door. A scale rested next to the chairs, and Lyla deduced that she was in a doctor's office.

She shut her eyes as tight as she could, angry that the world had pried them open again. She didn't want to be awake. Her best friend had just been hit by a car. Lyla had watched her fly through the air and smack into pavement. If Tara were alive, it would be no small miracle.

No, Lyla told herself. Tara couldn't be dead. She was her best friend. She was the Ying to her Yang, her opposite, the one who completed her. Lyla was the athlete, Tara the brains. Lyla was the uber-popular one with the dates and the parties, Tara the calming force of Netflix and pajamas. No, Lyla needed Tara. Tara could not be dead.

The door opened and a man in a white doctor's jacket and khakis walked in.

"I see you're up," he said tiredly below a pair of glasses. He attempted a rueful smile and took a deep breath. "How are you feeling?"

"Tara. Where's Tara? Where's my friend? Where's Tara?"

The doctor pursed his lips and narrowed his eyes, pausing for what seemed like hours.

"She's...not here. She was taken to John's Hopkins in Baltimore. That's all I know."

Lyla looked at him and knew he was telling the truth. She nodded numbly.

"I'll get your parents. They've been waiting for you to wake up."

The doctor strode out, leaving the door open, and within seconds her parents came rushing in.

"Are you OK, baby?" her mother asked, cradling her head in her arms. "Are you alright?"

Her father took her left hand in his and squeezed it reassuringly.

"Don't worry," he said. "You won't even have to miss a game. You were barely even hurt. Just a couple scrapes from the fall."

Lyla felt her insides boil. Basketball? Her father was thinking about basketball? She ripped her hand out of his and smacked him as hard across the face as she could muster. The left side of his face instantly flushed a beat red. His mustache twitched uncontrollably.

"Mike," hissed her mother. "Let her be for just a second."

He stormed out of the room.

"He...asked...about...basketball?" Lyla spat. She was sobbing again, more out of a disgust than anything. "Basketball?

"Freaking basketball? Where's Tara? Where's my best friend? Where is she, mom? Where's Tara?"

In that moment, Sue realized just how little she knew about her daughter. She had no idea what to say, no earthly clue how much Tara French meant to her. Lyla had talked of her warmly often but Sue had never gone out of her way to meet the girl. In fact, she realized, Tara was the only friend Lyla ever cared to mention.

Everything else was college and basketball, basketball and college. Sue assumed Lyla had good grades but never asked for a report card. Her Lyla was smart, wasn't she? Mike wanted the Storm house to be a basketball house, so that's the way it was. Now, she was looking into the blood-shot eyes of a daughter she realized she barely knew and was supposed to tell her...tell her what, exactly? There was no way Tara was going to make it. Sue knew that. Maybe honesty, she thought, is best.

"Lyla, baby," she whispered, holding her daughter close. "It's not good, baby. It's not good at all. I don't think...I don't think Tara is going to make it, baby."

Lyla buried her head in her mother's chest and screamed until her throat could scream no longer and cried until her eyes had no more tears left in them and the world went cold and black again.

Maryland Christian Athletic Conference Standings

Boys

St. Andrew's 10-0

Covenant Prep 9-1

Bishop O'Connell 7-3

Bishop McNamara 5-5

Good Counsel 4-6

Bishop Ireton 4-6

Gonzaga 3-7

St. Anselm's 0-10

Girls

Covenant Prep 9-1

Bishop O'Connell 9-1

Gonzaga 7-3

St. Andrew's 5-5

Bishop McNamara 5-5

Good Counsel 4-6

St. Anselm's 2-8

Bishop Ireton 2-8

CHAPTER 12

Time froze in Gaithersburg. The students went to school but weren't there. Teachers spoke but didn't teach. Periods came and passed and nobody seemed to notice. They walked through the hallways like zombies. Occasionally, someone would offer a fake smile. It wouldn't be returned. Laughs were hollow, disingenuous.

Three school days went by and Tara's specter hung over the school like a fog. Coach Koontz had called a team meeting the Monday after the accident and told the girls she'd be on the court for afternoon practice at 4 o'clock, as always. They didn't need to show, or even practice if they did, but she'd be there for them.

A few dragged themselves in. Nadia Blake, the starting center, was there, as were Gabby Browning and DeDe Trier, Lyla's backcourt mates. That was all. They sat together at midcourt and cried. Coach Koontz sat with them but didn't cry. Someone had to be strong for the kids, though she wasn't sure if she was up to the task.

Nobody had seen Lyla since the accident. She skipped school. Her parents never checked her attendance anyway, so she'd leave as normal, not saying a word, and drive aimlessly around town for an hour, no music, lost in a sea of empty thoughts, until her parents had left for work and she could retreat to the safety of her bedroom, where she'd pull the covers over her head like a child, curl up into a ball, and cry herself to sleep.

She didn't understand. Couldn't understand. So she didn't try to. She became a recluse. She tried to pick up a basketball but felt nauseous at the touch. It reminded her of Tara. It reminded her of how Tara had always wanted Lyla to teach her how to shoot just like her, to dribble just like her, to dominate just like her. Yet Tara's parents never allowed her to come to the gym before school, because their little genius needed her sleep so as not to let her grades slip. Lyla whipped the ball against the wall and watched as it shattered her dozens of carefully arranged trophies.

The boys team didn't know what to do, either. They had suffered through their own tragedy and moved on accordingly. The death of Coach had shaken the community, but the resurgence of the team had given the town of Gaithersburg new life, a purpose. Now, in the matter of just a few weeks, Gaithersburg and Covenant Prep High School were burdened with its second death.

They had no reason not to play. It just felt…wrong. Even the sound of leather smacking on wood, once the sound of Gaithersburg's pulse, was somehow lifeless. The echoes reverberating on the gym wall sounded sinister in a way. Coach Snyder canceled Monday's practice after an hour of listless running through the motions.

"Take tomorrow off, too," he said. "Get your heads straight. Come back Wednesday. We have out of conference games this week: Landon on Thursday, Bullis on Friday—two games we should have no problem winning if our minds are right and our heads are there."

The boys did win, thumping Landon by 30 on a 36-point night from Jared and blasting Bullis by 17 on an oddly-prolific evening from Brandon Thompson, who scored 18 and dished out 13 assists.

The girls forfeited both. Coach Koontz kept practices voluntary and every day Nadia and Gabby and DeDe would show up, sit at midcourt and stare, occasionally whispering or murmuring. After an hour, they'd leave. Still, no one had seen or heard from Lyla Storm. She had told her dad that she went to the doctor's and had pneumonia. Mike raised an eyebrow but didn't question it.

"Better to stay at home and not play then," he said. "That way your stats per game won't suffer. Let's get you healthy and back on the court again."

It made her nauseous, talking to her father.

Lyla hated funerals. Always had. The optimistic like to look at them as celebrations of life. She thought this sickening. Tara's was scheduled for Saturday afternoon. She hadn't even managed to make it to school in what was now nine school days. How could she possibly attend her best friend's funeral? She couldn't be gone. This was some sick joke. They'd be back at Snickerdoodles in a few days. Tony would get them the usual. Lyla would talk about the list. Tara would fuss over boys and grades. This was how life worked. So no, she wasn't going to watch as the only girl who had taken the time to get to know Lyla Storm was lowered six feet into the ground. It wasn't real. She'd hide from it, the truth. If this past week had taught her one thing, it's that she was rather talented at vanishing.

A knock. Who could possibly be knocking? Lyla slipped out of bed and walked to her bedroom window, where, if she looked down at just the right angle, she could usually make out a visitor if she recognized their build. She didn't need the angle though. That car, the green Infiniti parked in front of the tree at the corner of the yard, was the dead giveaway: Coach Koontz. Lyla dabbed her eyes with a cold washcloth in an attempt to reduce the swelling from all of her crying.

What would she say? Koontz wouldn't buy her pneumonia bit. How could she explain to her coach why she hadn't been to school for nearly two weeks, hadn't been there to grade her tests, hadn't been at practice when the team needed her most, hadn't returned any of the 15 voicemails Koontz left her, hadn't registered a pulse to anyone outside of the Storm household since Tara lost hers permanently?

She hesitated at the door.

"Lyla Storm," Koontz's booming voice called out. "I know you're in there. I saw the curtain move when you walked by, anyway. If you don't open up, I'm coming in. I'll kick the gosh darn door down if I have to and I'd really rather not do that."

Lyla unlocked the door with a soft click and walked hastily to the family room. She collapsed on the couch and waited. Gosh, the effort from leaving her bed was exhausting.

"You look like hell, darlin'," Coach Koontz said as her way of greeting. Koontz was, as always, decked out in Prep sweats: red sweat pants, blue sweatshirt, gray Prep basketball shoes.

Lyla could feel her eyes surveying her, looking her over. Koontz noted her gaunt face, significantly leaner arms, swollen eyes, greasy hair.

"Good Lord, almighty, Lyla. Have you eaten? Have you showered? Have you even left the house?"

No answer. She sat down and sighed, a heavy, tired sigh, as if she were carrying a great weight and was just happy to finally sit down.

"Look, I know you loved that girl. I did, too. She may not have been much of a basketball player but daggummit if every player had the heart she did we'd never lose a game. She was smart and had a heart of gold. Still, Lyla, no matter how good a person is, I don't care if it's the president or Michael Jordan or Coach Stottlemyer or Tara French, the world does not stop turning when they move on. You need to realize you are not doing her, yourself, your team or your family, any favors by holing up here, by yourself, wallowing in pity. I hate to have to resort to tough love in a situation as delicate and tragic as this one but, honey, you need to pick yourself up and move on with it."

Lyla's insides were hot with rage, though she couldn't say why. Everything Coach Koontz had said made perfect sense. Yet how could she move on? How was she supposed to? How was she…how was she supposed to do anything?

"Coach," her voice was barely a whisper. She hadn't spoken much in two weeks. It felt strange to use those muscles again. "I don't know how. What am I supposed to do?"

Koontz sidled up next to her and threw a comforting, muscular arm around her.

"You just live your life a little better each day. Live a little more like Tara French, like Coach Stottlemyer. Live because they can't, because in here, whatever it is you've been doing this past week, is hardly any better than dying, Lyla. Live. That's it. That, honey, is how you move on."

Lyla nodded. She was numb. She didn't respond, though she didn't really have to. Her nod seemed to do the job.

"The funeral is tomorrow. If you're not there, you're off the team."

Lyla nodded. Koontz rose to leave but Lyla pulled her back down.

"Coach?" she said, hugging her close. "I love you."

"Love you too, sweetheart. Be brave, OK? I'll see you tomorrow."

The cemetery was 45 minutes away, tucked in a grove in neighboring Quince Orchard. Lyla had pulled up 20 minutes early, waiting in her Lexus, attempting to steady her breathing. This would be the last time Tara French was not six feet below the Earth. Lyla closed her eyes and shuddered.

The next moments are fragments. Thirsty. Lyla was so darn thirsty. Black coats. Black dresses. Mr. French. Teammates. Family. Tears. Can someone get her some freaking water? A coffin. An empty six-foot rectangle. Her best friend. A filled six-foot rectangle. Crying. Coach Koontz's arm linking with hers.

Water. She wanted water. Needed water. Her throat was scratchy. Her eyes must have stolen the last drops of liquid from her body because her mouth had none of it.

Coach Koontz handed her a cup of steaming something. Smelled like coffee. Lyla didn't like coffee. It tasted wonderful. It burned going down. Felt good, perfect even. She hadn't felt warm since that day. Oh, no. That day. She began thinking about it. The cars. The squeal of rubber tires on asphalt. Tara's body catapulting through the air.

Crying again, Lyla crumpled to the cold, hard earth, collapsing onto her butt like a child. She closed her eyes and shook with sobs for an amount of time she will never know, only that when she opened them, only Mr. French and Coach Koontz remained. He was sitting there with her and she discovered that her head was on his thin, bony shoulder.

"I'm so sorry," she managed to croak, her throat cracking with each word. "I didn't mean to...I...sorry."

"Shh," Mr. French cooed, squeezing her shoulder. "Shh."

They sat there for 10, 30, 45 minutes. Lyla didn't know. Mr. French was one of the few people in whom Lyla had ever confided. He was more a father to her than her own father. She talked to him about grades and boys and dresses and teachers. They rarely, if ever, talked about basketball. When the topic did come up, it was when Lyla introduced it and it was always about Tara, how well she played, how much Lyla loved watching her play.

For the first time in their many conversations, Mr. French was the one to bring up basketball.

"Lyla," he said, and she could smell stale cigarettes on his breath. She didn't know he smoked. "You need to play. The girls need you to play. The school needs you to play. This town needs you to play.

"I've talked to Coach Koontz." He motioned to where she was standing, looking down upon them, focused and serious, hands on her hips. God, how could she be so strong? "She's right. The world stops for no one person. Not even my Tara."

"I don't know how."

Snow began to flurry from the gray sky above.

How could she know how to resume life as normal? Lyla was the heart of the team. This much was obvious. Without her, the team would not survive. It would merely exist, a piece of nothing. Tara was the soul, an enigma. As a soul is within a human, Tara did not exist in the physical, the box scores and stats and newspaper stories and offense and defense, but she breathed life and character and goofiness into that team. She gave them personality. When the girls would fight, as girls do, Tara would invite them over for donuts. She would tell them not to worry about gaining weight, because the hole in the center of donuts are 100 percent fat free. They would laugh and laugh and forget about whatever petty problems had bothered them before. So yes, Lyla was the heart, and a team cannot exist without a heart. But the existential soul, Tara's role, the one that was harder to define and even more difficult to see, Lyla did not believe the team could go on without that either.

"Sure you know how," Mr. French said. "You just don't know how to play for someone or something other than yourself."

The blunt honesty of the comment startled Lyla.

"You've never needed to. You are the team. Always have been. Probably always will be. But this isn't about the team anymore, is it? This is about much more. You are playing for the memory of my daughter, just as Kevin is playing for the memory of his father. You are both playing to keep this town, and yourselves, sane."

She wasn't sure she enjoyed being compared to Kevin, even if the comparison fit.

"That's a lot to ask of some teenage kids, I know. You can stop playing and feel sorry for yourself and I'm sure nobody would blame you. But know this: You are doing yourself no favors by doing that and you aren't honoring Tara in any way. I know that what you want to do more than anything is to honor my daughter. I know how good you were to her. I know what you meant to her and what she meant to you. So play, Lyla. Play the game that Tara will never be able to play again. Help get this town back on its feet.

"Listen, basketball isn't life. No matter what people tell you around here, it isn't. But it's a way to find our place in life, isn't it? So find your place, Lyla."

He squeezed her tight and rose to his feet. He turned, pulled his black coat close, and before he walked out into the cool, snow-filled afternoon, he placed a bible at her feet.

"Read the page I have marked for you."

He kissed her on the forehead and disappeared with Coach Koontz into the snowy afternoon.

Lyla fingered the black bible and flipped open to the page Mr. French had dog-eared for her. It was to the Book of Isaiah, and he had highlighted the verse 61:3: "And provide for those who grieve in Zion—to bestow on them a crown of beauty instead of ashes, the oil of joy instead of mourning, and a garment of praise instead of a spirit of despair."

Lyla closed her eyes and hugged the bible. The verse was, as Mr. French no doubt knew, perfect. Her butt had grown numb from the cold. She took a deep inhale, closed her eyes and pulled herself up.

The team needed its heart to begin beating again. Lyla had work to do.

CHAPTER 13

The alarm erupted to life, splitting the 5 a.m. serenity with its usual relentless and painful beeping. Kevin rolled over and slammed it, groaned once, twice, inhaled, exhaled, fell—literally, fell, as it was the only way he could summon himself out of bed at such an ungodly hour anymore—and lay on the floor for a beat.

The regular season was nearly at an end. Just two games remained, both likely to be easy wins, with struggling Bishop Ireton and 10-6 out of conference Capitol Christian on the schedule. The toll of playing 16 games, in which Prep had rolled up a record of 13-

3, practicing four hours a day for nearly three months with nary a day off, and waking up at this time of day for each of those days, takes a toll on a 17-year-old kid.

He rubbed the sleep out of his eyes and sat up, Indian-style, on his blue carpet. The sun wasn't yet up and Kevin had learned to relish the peaceful, pre-dawn blackness. It was a welcome reprieve from the gloom that hung over Prep. A yawn stretched out of his lungs as he rubbed his hands down his legs, both to warm them and to take stock of his various bumps and bruises. A charge against St. Anselm's had left a nasty, storm-cloud colored mark on his left knee. A dive in another blowout of Good Counsel resulted in his elbow blowing up to the size of a softball. A collision with the center from St. Andrew's, in which Prep lost again but only by two, had left him with a serious hurting in his abdomen. Frankly, he ached everywhere. Such was the toll of a basketball season.

Still, there was so much more weighing on him than a few nicks and sore muscles and joints. Kevin would have been eternally grateful to have just a bruise here, a cut there, a stress fracture in a foot. Two deaths, instead, had been added to the ledger this season. The wound of his father's passing had finally begun to scab over when Tara's car accident blew it wide open again. Mentally, Kevin, like the town, had little left in the tank. Physically, Kevin, like the town, didn't know if they could or should move on as they always had, with basketball at the forefront and the rest of life two or three priorities behind.

He had changed his routine. Whether the rest of Gaithersburg did, he wasn't sure. If they didn't, they were stuck and life, as he had been reminded often by his late father, waits for no one. So he did what he now did every morning: He turned over onto his knees and bowed so his forehead rested on his bed, his hands clasped in prayer. Prior to the death of Coach, Kevin hadn't prayed much. Didn't have much faith in the Big Man Upstairs, as his dad referred to God. How could he? This so called benevolent "God" had let his father suffer for a year then stole him away. The thought of it had once made Kevin detest any sign of religion. After his father passed, though, he did what many do when searching for an answer to a question without one: He turned to faith, seeking the help and guidance his mother had attempted to steer him toward for the past year. Praying had become a cathartic release. He didn't understand how speaking to an invisible presence in the sky, one he still wasn't entirely sure he believed existed, could offer such equanimity to his troubled mind, yet faith isn't meant to be understood, is it? It's actually sort of the point.

He thanked the Lord for blessing him with another day. He thanked his father for watching over him, as he figured he would be, unless there was basketball in Heaven, in which case his dad might be coaching up there, too. Though he couldn't believe it himself, he prayed for Lyla. He hadn't seen her at school since Tara's accident. He had never worried much about Lyla. Why would he? She had everything. He couldn't help but be a little concerned. He'd never seen the girl like this. He closed with the Lord's prayer—*Our*

Father, who art in Heaven... — and rolled onto his feet, jogged downstairs and left for the gym.

Kevin couldn't remember the last time he saw that car, the sleek, gunmetal Lexus, parked in the spot second from the stairs leading to the school. It seemed like forever. It seemed like yesterday. Time had become so distorted in Gaithersburg.

Kevin parked his Sable in its standard spot and paused in front of Lyla's Lexus. Frost had begun to cake the windshield again. It must have been there for a bit. His breath blew out in a plume in front of him, hanging there like a specter in the cold morning. Lyla had been devastated by Tara's death. Kevin understood. He and death had become close acquaintances. Coach's death had been foreseen, as scheduled as death could be. Tara's was dreadfully abrupt.

He wasn't sure why, but he slid his hand along the sleek frame of the Lexus, almost to make sure it was really there. Kevin figured Lyla to be done for the season, possibly her career. She would never be able to separate basketball from Tara, which is another way of saying she would never be able to separate basketball from death. He knew the feeling. Sure enough, his hand felt the freezing surface of the Lexus and it was confirmed: Lyla was, indeed, here.

The gym was warm, a welcome change from the white layer of snow outside. Kevin paused at the entrance, watching silently as his old nemesis, the haughty Lyla Storm, the girl who had picked on him since fifth grade for being too slow or short or chubby or vertically challenged, poured in shot after shot. She never paused, in perpetual motion. Kevin wondered if she thought if she stopped shooting, the ghost of Tara might seep into her consciousness again.

Kevin wasn't sure how to enter the gym. Say hi? No, he hadn't spoken to Lyla in weeks and when he had, it wasn't pleasant, all trash talk and bragging. Walk past her as he had in the first two months of the season, saying nothing? That seemed somehow wrong. This was a girl who had just lost her best friend, who had disappeared. No, he couldn't do that, either.

So he let the door do the greeting for him, allowing it to slam with an audible, echoing whack. Lyla jumped, startled. She turned. Kevin could tell from across the court that her eyes were red and puffy, and her nose was scarlet, presumably from blowing it so many times. He took note of her considerably leaner arms, her pronounced cheekbones. She hadn't eaten much since Tara's accident. Kevin knew Lyla had claimed pneumonia was keeping her out of school. The entire school knew this was not true, though nobody, not the teachers, nurses or principals, would dare call her on it. Anyway, seeing her dilapidated state, she did look like a girl who was legitimately suffering from pneumonia.

She smiled weakly. Kevin smiled back. He walked stiffly and awkwardly to the rack of basketballs at midcourt, unsure of what to say, do or feel. He picked one up. Put it down. Glanced sideways at Lyla. Then he did something he had never done before, an act so simple, so routine, that we take it for granted every day, but something we crave, whether we know it or not: Kevin wrapped his arms around her and he hugged her. It was a long, deep, tight hug, one Kevin wasn't sure he had in him for Lyla, or anyone, for that matter. He had never hugged anyone the way he hugged Lyla Storm that morning.

Lyla buried her head in his sweatshirt. She was hot and wet from sweat but Kevin could feel a distinct sort of wetness from tears beginning to puddle onto his sweatshirt. She shook from crying and Kevin held her tighter.

"It's alright," he whispered. He stroked her hair. "It's all gonna be alright. You're not alone."

The words sounded stupid coming out of him. He hadn't rehearsed them in his head. They just sort of clumsily tumbled out.

He wasn't sure how long they stood there, embracing at midcourt. A minute? Two? Ten? Kevin didn't know what to feel, didn't know what to think or say, how tight to hold his arms around her or where to place his hands. He didn't know whether to close his eyes or where his head should go. In that moment, all Kevin knew was that he wanted to hold Lyla Storm for as long as it took. Eventually, she released him and looked at him, blue eyes especially brilliant through the puddles of tears. Kevin couldn't help but think of how beautiful she looked.

"How'd you do it?" she whispered.

"Just put one foot in front of the other until you learn to walk again."

She nodded, as if that explained everything, put her head on Kevin's chest once more then turned, picked up her basketball and began shooting.

Kevin picked up a ball from the rack, glanced back at Lyla one more time, strode towards his hoop and began to shoot.

Life had returned to Covenant Prep.

CHAPTER 14

Even with their undefeated start, the girls team had forfeited too many games—six in all, plus one for the game the night of the accident—in the wake of Tara's death to earn a high seed in the playoffs.

Bishop O'Connell, armed with two sharp-shooting sisters by the names of Katie and Megan O'Brien, had only lost two games, both to Prep, yet had still finished 14-2 to take the No. 1 seed, even if they lost both their remaining games this week. If Lyla and the girls won both of their remaining games, which was no longer a sure thing given the circumstances, they would get the three seed, behind O'Connell and Gonzaga.

Nobody was concerned about what playoff seed they got or whom they beat or how many points so and so scored. The town of Gaithersburg just wanted basketball, its reliable vehicle through all times tough and basketball was exactly what Kevin, Jared and the Covenant Prep boys delivered.

On Tuesday, they traveled to Bishop Ireton. The boys' result was a foregone conclusion. Ireton had been awful all season, winning only a handful of games against the bottom feeders. The Stags had only lost twice since the passing of Coach, something that wouldn't change, as if Ireton hadn't even been on the schedule in the first place.

Kevin came out with fire on his fingertips, burying four 3-pointers in the first quarter and assisting on two others to Brandon Thompson. Prep led 24-4 and Coach Snyder was already unloading the bench. Jared remained in to get his reps up and he took over the second quarter much as Kevin had the first. A twisting layup through the lane kicked off his onslaught, which preceded a pair of fast break dunks off of steals, a pull-up 3-pointer from the right wing, a blocked shot, a gorgeous behind the back pass to a streaking Garrett Kron and an ill-advised up-and-under reverse layup that somehow counted for two points and sent Snyder through the gamut of emotions ranging from rage to shock to relieved laughter.

If any team was going to stop Prep, which was doubtful anyone not named St. Andrew's could, it was not Ireton. The Stags led 58-14 at halftime. Kevin didn't see the court once after the first quarter. Jared didn't step foot on it after halftime. With Brandon and Garrett leading the way, Prep stomped Ireton 82-38 and sealed up their No. 1 seed over St. Andrew's.

The Lions of St. Andrew's had been putting together a perfectly solid season. As they always did, they had loaded their schedule with strong, nationally-ranked out of conference opponents and lost accordingly, weakening their record to 12-4 but strengthening their overall play.

Jack Miller, who had torched Kevin in the season opener, was without a shred of doubt going to be named Player of the Year. Kevin and Jared knew it. Miller was averaging 30 points per game and shooting at a torrid 65 percent. Nobody could stop him. Kevin wasn't entirely sure he could, either.

The only time Kevin would get another shot at Miller would be in the championship game. Because the Stags had sealed up the one seed, St. Andrew's subsequently took the two. They would be on opposite sides of the bracket.

As expected, the boys game had little fanfare. The Prep denizens knew there wasn't much point in watching a massacre and had timed their arrival for the start of the girls game, for which there was a strange collective hesitancy in the air, as if everybody were holding their breath but didn't want the person standing next to them to know. Nobody knew what to expect from Lyla Storm and the Covenant Prep girls, which was an odd sensation considering, for the past three years, everybody had known exactly what to expect from Lyla Storm and the Covenant Prep girls.

In the locker room, where the sounds of several hundred fans could be heard reverberating through the walls, Lyla put her head down in prayer. This wasn't new to her. She had worn her cross necklace every single day since her grandmother gifted it to her at Lyla's confirmation in fifth grade. Despite her parents not being big churchgoers, Lyla still made time every Sunday and prayed before bed every night. What she said when she bowed her head, however, was different. She had never prayed for herself before, always asking for safety for all of the players, for the Lord to bless them with a clean, friendly game. Tara had joined her in this pre-game ritual since they first began playing together. This time, she wasn't too unselfish to ask for guidance for herself, if God could just help her through the game and keep her focused on anything but Tara. To keep her from crying in the middle of the court. Lyla needed help. She was no longer too afraid to ask for it.

Coach Koontz ended all thoughts there. "Alright, fifteen minutes!" she barked. Lyla kissed her cross necklace, tucked it into her red gym bag and trotted to where Koontz and the team gathered in the moldy Ireton locker room.

"I know how y'all must feel, trust me. I coached Tara French for years and years. Loved that girl. Y'all have been through a lot. I wouldn't have blamed ya if ya called it quits this season but I'm glad you didn't, because now we can be so much more than just a basketball team to this town. We can be so much more than a group of girls who puts an orange ball through a hoop and wins a few games. Alongside our boys, who just kicked some serious tail, by the way, we can be an inspiration like no other this town has seen. I'm proud of you, proud beyond words, girls."

Koontz paused as she sought eye contact with every single one of her players before her. "Tonight, tomorrow, the rest of the season, we play for Tara. I want y'all to wear these."

Koontz reached into the right pocket of her black dress pants and produced red patches with Tara's number 35 and "French" sewed onto the bottom in blue writing.

"Just peel the back and stick them onto your left shoulder, just above your hearts, where Tara's memory will always belong. She's up there watching us right now, you know, hoping for a blowout so she could get in and run the offense wrong and probably miss a few layups."

A few players laughed. Even Lyla caught herself grinning, then cupped her hands over her mouth, as if she had just committed a crime. Should she be laughing right now? Was that right? Lyla looked at Koontz, who nodded, smiling, apparently able to read her thoughts—yes, smiling was OK.

"So come on. Put your hands in."

The girls formed a tight circle around Koontz, placing their hands on top of one another until Koontz was the only one left.

"Prep on three. One, two, THREE..."

"Prep!" they yelled. As the 11 other Stags charged out of the locker room, Koontz put a hand on Lyla's chest.

"Take off your jersey, Storm."

Lyla paused, a little stunned. Was Koontz really about to bench her? Not let her play right now? Koontz, always in Lyla's head, laughed at what must have been a shocked facial expression.

"No, you dope, you're still playing. I want to give you something. Take off your jersey."

Lyla reluctantly removed her red jersey and tossed it to the floor, the blue lettering with "STORM" written on the back shining back up at them. She looked down at her body, which was covered only by a blue sports bra. She could see the outline of a few ribs. Gosh, she really had gotten skinny, hadn't she?

"Here."

Koontz handed her a different jersey, brand new by the smell and untarnished look of it. Lyla unfolded it and ran her eyes over it. When she flipped it over and looked at the number, she nearly fell over.

A blue number 35 stared back at her. Tara's number. Lyla turned the jersey to the back and "FRENCH" was written at the top instead of "STORM."

Her mind raced. No way. Sorry, coach. Can't do it. Lyla tried to push the jersey back at Koontz but the coach wouldn't have it, gently easing the jersey back into her star player's hands.

"Wear it, for her, for the French family, for the school. They need you, Lyla. They need you."

Koontz walked out, leaving Lyla alone with her thoughts. She sat down on a cold metal bench, turning the jersey over and over in her hands. She closed her eyes, smelled it, stupidly thinking it might carry the vanilla scent of her late best friend. It didn't. Of course it didn't. Her friend was dead.

She thought about what Koontz had said—"Wear it for her."

Tara had always told Lyla she wanted to be just like her—the looks, the athletics, the boys, the popularity. Lyla had never told Tara she would trade places with Tara, the one with the loving family and the freedom to pursue her own dreams, in a heartbeat. This was Lyla's chance genuinely to honor her best friend in the only way she knew how.

Coach Koontz was right.

Wasn't she always?

Lyla took a deep inhale and pulled the jersey over her head, tucking it into her waistband. She closed her eyes and rose, returning to basketball, returning to life.

CHAPTER 15

It was a strange feeling for Lyla, to have these nerves. Out on the court, where she had always felt most comfortable, she could now feel her heartbeat in her temples, ears, wrists, neck and chest. She wiped her palms on her shorts 10, 12, 15 times but the coating of sweat couldn't be dried. Even if they were as dry as a desert, they still shook like a loose rim in a dunk contest. She took a warm-up jump shot from the right wing and missed the hoop entirely. When layup lines began, she missed her first four, hammering them off the backboard. She chucked a pass so hard at DeDe that it nearly knocked the little point guard over.

Coach Koontz saw this from her spot on the bench and didn't know what to think, do or say. She had dealt with a great many things in her 10 years of coaching. Players had fights with parents, breakups with boyfriends, lost beloved grandparents. Some would become chronically overwhelmed with nerves in big games. Others would shut down if they received a bad grade on a test or didn't get into their first choice of college. Koontz had always figured out a way to get her players to focus on basketball. But she had never coached an athlete quite as peculiar as Lyla Storm.

Lyla was a curious blend of brashness and insecurity, the former, she guessed, exaggerated to mask the latter. Koontz knew she was one of the few who Lyla allowed behind that flawless façade she had so carefully manufactured. Tara, as far as Koontz knew, was the only other. It must be difficult to lose 50 percent of the people on the planet whom you trust. Now, Koontz, Lyla and the Covenant Prep girls were out of time. It was either Lyla worked out the ghost of Tara's death that haunted her, or the Stags' season, and possibly even Lyla's career, was over.

The horn sounded, warning both teams they had one minute of warmups left. She whistled them over. Lyla, normally front and center of the huddle, often the one hollering out orders and setting up the offense and defense while Koontz monitored from the outside, stood behind Nadia, the center. Koontz could barely see her.

"Lyla!" Koontz yelled.

Nadia turned, allowing Lyla to slip inside the huddle.

"This is your team. Get them ready."

Lyla froze.

"Um," she stammered. Her hands began to sweat uncontrollably. Her voice shook. She could feel her heartbeat hammering in her ears, even harder than before. *What do I say? What do I say?*

The weight of it seemed to crush her. Her vision narrowed. Her voice sounded foreign. Sweat, so much sweat. And she was so damn thirsty again, just like...oh, God, she began thinking about it: the funeral, Tara, her best friend dying. Tears formed at the corners of her eyes. She still tried it.

"Guys...I..." A lump formed in her throat, as if she had just swallowed a tennis ball.

Koontz put a reassuring hand on her shoulder and gently ushered her next to Nadia.

"OK, here's what we're gonna do. We're starting DeDe, Nadia, Gabby, Brittany and Katie. Lyla, take a minute to gather yourself. You'll be in when you think you're ready. There's no shame in sitting out for the first time in your life."

Koontz smiled and the girls offered a courtesy laugh and looked at Lyla, who was staring absentmindedly at the floor, completely numb. Gabby and Brittany Browning, sisters who had never been particularly close with Lyla but who were teammates all the same, shared a worried glance.

"We're gonna play man to man on defense. They don't have a ball handler, so Brittany and Gabby and DeDe, I want you pressuring them until they pop. They'll turn it over. As soon as they do, take off. I want you to run their legs off. By the time the second half comes around, they'll be so tired they'll be thanking us for taking the ball off their hands. C'mon now, bring it in."

"Oh, and Nadia," Koontz continued, eyeing her enormous center, "don't worry about keeping up with all those little guards running around. Just stay in the lane and be big."

She winked and Nadia grinned widely. It was a role she was quite willing to play. Koontz put a hand in the center of the huddle and one by one the players threw theirs in the middle.

"Listen, I know this won't be easy. Nobody expected it to be, especially not me. Just go out there and remember why you're playing this game—to have a little fun. So go have some daggum fun, will ya? Stags on three. One, two, three...

"Stags!" they screamed and the five starters trotted out onto the court.

Lyla slumped at the end of the bench, confused and alone.

As always, Nadia, being 6-foot-4 and a good head above every other girl who attempted to guard her, won the jump ball, flipping it back to DeDe. The little point guard shot up the court, zipping through Ireton defenders, all the way to the basket. The wonderful thing about DeDe Trier's game was she could fly up and down with the speed that had helped her win state in the 100-meter dash last spring. The bad thing about DeDe's game was that she could not control that speed for the life of her.

Her layup attempt hit the backboard so hard the ball landed at the free throw line and an Ireton guard scooped it up, pausing to let her teammates get down the court before bringing it up.

Then the game came. To. A. Stop.

Ireton did what any well-coached, severely undermanned team would do: It held the ball. The Musketeers ran what is called a shuffle offense. It has a series of three cuts and then it restarts, running the same three cuts over and over and over until the defense falls asleep and allows an easy shot. With the absence of a shot clock and Lyla, the best defender in the state who no team could run a stall-ball offense against because she would find a way to steal it, Ireton could eat up chunks of clock without the Stags even touching the ball.

On the bench, Koontz seethed. "Pressure! Pressure!"

DeDe was the only one with the proper combination of speed, athleticism and basketball IQ to put any turnover-inducing pressure on an Ireton guard, a fact that was not lost on the Musketeers. They avoided DeDe, cycling the offense through repeatedly without her mark ever touching the ball. She just set pick after pick while her teammates ran through the motions with little intent on scoring a basket until the offense had been running so long that Nadia evidently grew disinterested. She trotted around a screen, not expecting her mark to actually call for the ball, but she did, and when her teammate dished her a pass what she found was a wide-open lane and no defender at the rim.

Two points, Ireton.

"Are you kiddin' me, Nadia?" Koontz screamed. "Are you freakin' kiddin' me?"

Lyla glanced at the clock. Four minutes had passed on one offensive possession. She felt a hint of anger. It was strange, experiencing an emotion other than a suffocating sadness. Anger felt lively. It felt red hot and full of life. It felt quite splendid. DeDe zipped down the court and forced another hurried shot, clanging it off the back rim. Nadia couldn't get her hands on the rebound and Ireton put on the brakes again.

"Just run your shuffle, girls," the Ireton coach, a tall lady with brown hair and the most monotonous voice Koontz thought she'd ever heard, said. "Worked last time."

They did. Over and over and over again, until it was Brittany, a 3-point specialist with a glaringly obvious disdain for defense, who was caught sleeping.

Four to nothing, Ireton. One minute remained.

DeDe sprinted full-speed down the court again, about to blow by another defender before she got tripped up and went skidding into the Prep bench, slamming next to Lyla's feet. Her defender followed her there.

"Guess you're not so hot now, hot shot," the Ireton guard spat, glaring at Lyla. "Your girlfriend's gone so you can't play no more? Poor whiddle baby."

She made a mock crying face at Lyla and there it went. Something inside Lyla snapped or clicked or whatever you'd like to call it but, oh, did Lyla Storm feel it go. She had never felt such a rage before in her life. Her face grew hot. She could physically feel the blood rushing through her veins. It was more than anger. This was a profound fury, a wildfire Lyla had no intent on corralling. She launched herself off the bench so fast her neighboring teammates fell backwards. She was nose to nose with the impetuous little Ireton player now, practically foaming at the mouth. She wanted to say something but instead smiled. It was a cold-blooded smile that would have made a grown man wilt and shrink and wish he had somewhere better to be, for anywhere would be better than directly in front of this 5-foot-10 maelstrom of hate and loathing and white hot pissed off teenage girl.

The refs intervened, separating the two and the Ireton player shrunk into the background, seeming to come to the conclusion she had just signed her team's death warrant. Lyla stomped onto the court. Her court. And she felt right at home.

"Who are you getting?" Koontz stammered at Lyla, shocked at the sudden burst of life from her star player.

"I don't care. Just tell somebody to get off my freakin' court."

Lyla's voice was steady again, icy, utterly terrifying.

Koontz smiled, though a small part of her was legitimately frightened for any Bishop Ireton player left on the court. She glanced over at Ireton's coach.

130

"Coach," she called. "I'd highly recommend you inform your players to never talk trash to Lyla Storm again. As in ever. This is not going to be pretty. And I am going to run this score up until the numbers don't go any higher."

Koontz motioned for DeDe to take a seat next to the bench she had just tumbled into and Lyla walked to midcourt grinning a wicked grin. The fans erupted, turning the Ireton gym from a library-like silence into a rollicking mass of teenage exuberance.

"Ly-La, Ly-La, Ly-La!" they chanted, clapping their hands in unison.

The ref handed Nadia the ball and blew the whistle. Game on.

Nadia inbounded it to Lyla and the whole gym was on its feet. She took two dribbles and pulled up from four feet beyond the 3-point line. It ripped through the net and a jet may as well have taken off inside the gym those fans roared so loud.

"Ly-La, Ly-La, Ly-La, Ly-La!" they screamed and Lyla screamed right back. She reared back her head, her ponytail waving to either side, and screamed to the heavens. She pounded her chest and cried to her fans, pulling the front of her jersey out to show the number 35 she proudly boasted on her chest.

Ireton tried to walk the ball up the court but Lyla was there. She hounded that stupid little point guard she loathed and the Musketeer panicked, picking up her dribble too soon and forcing a pass to the middle, directly into the waiting hands of Gabby, who caught it and flipped it to Lyla, who scored a layup.

Another eruption came from the Stag faithful.

The buzzer sounded, and to a casual passerby it must have seemed the most ridiculous thing, a gym exploding with raw, unfiltered emotion for a scoreboard that read 5-4 after the first quarter. But it was so much more. This was the return of Lyla Storm. This was the tribute to Tara French. This was the collective sound of the town of Gaithersburg taking its first steps, moving on.

"Huddle up!" Lyla screamed at her teammates. Her eyes were wild, a white fire smoldering among icy blue.

"I don't care if you have to tackle one of those stupid little girls, they will not score a point the rest of this half. I don't care if you claw them, push them, pull their hair, whatever. Foul out if you have to. I'll play them one on five if it comes to it. By the end of this half, they better be so scared to play basketball against us they don't come out of the freakin' locker room."

There's something about emotion in sports that's contagious. None of the Stags had heard what the Musketeer point guard said to Lyla. But Lyla had abruptly become incensed, so they became incensed.

Prep began with the ball and Lyla walked the ball down and buried a 3 without hesitation.

"What? Nobody going to guard me? Not even you, hot stuff?" she sneered at the Ireton guard. Lyla turned to the Ireton coach, who seemed smaller, somehow, than she had before.

"What? Don't have anybody to guard me? Too scared to send somebody out to the three-point line?"

Prep, with Lyla back in all of her swaggering glory, sprung its deadly press as soon as Ireton inbounded the ball and six straight times a Stag stole it. In a matter of four minutes, a 5-4, uncomfortably close game, snowballed into a 20-4 blowout. There would be no letup. Lyla was called for a technical foul when she got tangled up with the Ireton center, who was far taller and considerably heavier, and slammed her to the floor.

"Is that really what you teach your players, coach?" the Ireton coach shouted, pointing an accusing finger at Koontz. "Real classy."

Koontz just smiled from her spot on the bench—she was no longer bothering to stand in such a rout—and shrugged.

"We have MMA nights on Tuesdays."

The two free throws Ireton was given from the technical foul were the only shots the Musketeers took the rest of the half. As Lyla requested, they didn't pass half court. By halftime, Prep had opened up a 40-5 lead—the Ireton point guard made one of those two free throws. Lyla was still maniacal, screaming at every Ireton player who got near her. Nadia and DeDe had to pull her by the jersey just to get her into the locker room.

"Don't you dare take me out of this game," Lyla told Koontz, as the coach was readying her halftime speech.

There are those chosen athletes who have a certain look about them. It's a controlled chaos, dangerously flirting with the line of a not-so-controlled chaos. It's wild and crazed, borderline animalistic. Lyla had that look. Her eyes burned with an intensity that verged on insanity. Her veins stood out like little blue tree roots, as if the blood in her body had missed the thrill of competition so much it felt the need to course through her tenfold that night. All Koontz could do was smile.

"Everybody else OK with Lyla staying in?"

They whooped in unanimous approval.

"Bring it in on me then," Lyla screamed.

The girls glanced around each other, and it still seemed so wrong to smile without their teammate, whose void in the huddle and in the halftime locker room was so poignantly felt. Then again, it felt so right to play this way in her name.

"Prep on three. One, two, three..."

"Prep!" they screamed.

Lyla didn't so much walk onto the court as she stormed, a bull let out of its pen and all she could see was red. She found the nearest Ireton player and stuck her nose with hers.

"This is going to be the worst sixteen minutes of your life," she hissed, and it was infinitely more terrifying than if she had screamed. "I hope you know that."

DeDe picked off a pass on the press and dished it to Lyla, who buried a 3-pointer.

"All freakin' night!" she bellowed, banging her chest with her fist, flashing the number 35 again. "All freakin' night, do not let them over half court. Not one single time."

Four more steals translated to 10 points for the Stags, who now held a 48-point lead and were still pressing. The Ireton coach called a timeout and charged over to Koontz.

"Is this what you teach your players? Is this sportsmanship? Is this basketball to you?"

Koontz, who stood a full head taller than the other woman, jumped off the bench and took two giant steps towards her so they stood chest to chest. She stared down at her.

"Do you teach your players to demean a dead girl?"

The Ireton coach wilted under Koontz's icy gaze.

"If you don't like the way this game is going, I suggest you walk off the court right now, because that's the way this is going to go until that clock turns to zeroes or the refs call it for a mercy rule."

The Ireton coach took a step back and nodded.

"Girls," she called over, her hands cupped. "Let's go. This game is over."

The Prep denizens, who had showed up in enormous numbers to see Lyla and the girls return, erupted.

"Na-na-na-na, na-na-na-na, hey hey hey, goooooodbyeeeee!" they chanted as the Musketeers did a walk of shame off their own court. "Na-na-na-na, na-na-na-na, hey hey hey, goooooodbyeeeee!"

Then Lyla and the Stags strode out, whooping into the night, celebrating for the first time in what seemed like a lifetime.

Maryland Christian Athletic Conference Standings

Boys

Covenant Prep 14-3

St. Andrew's 13-4

Bishop O'Connell 12-5

Bishop McNamara 10-7

Good Counsel 10-7

Bishop Ireton 4-13

Gonzaga 2-15

St. Anselm's 1-16

Girls

Bishop O'Connell 15-2

Gonzaga 13-4

Covenant Prep 10-7

St. Andrew's 9-8

Bishop McNamara 8-9

Good Counsel 7-10

St. Anselm's 2-15

Bishop Ireton 1-16

CHAPTER 16

The playoff brackets were released on a Saturday, the day after each team had played its final regular season game and two days before the start of playoffs. Kevin sat at his computer in his room, Mandy bouncing on his lap, anxiously waiting. He must have refreshed his computer screen 100 times before the skeleton of a bracket finally filled out with school names and seeding numbers.

When Covenant Prep's name materialized at the top of the bracket in the slot next to the number one seed, he jumped out of his chair so quickly he knocked it over and sent Mandy crashing to the floor, letting out an enormous whoop as he did. Never mind that it was a foregone conclusion Prep had locked up the top seed. This was the town of Gaithersburg, where basketball took on a status that verged on deity. Kevin was going to celebrate. In fact, Kevin was so busy celebrating he had completely forgotten about his girlfriend, who was sporting an impressive red lump on her forehead from slamming into the desk.

"Kev!" she wailed. "That hurt!"

Kevin cared. Of course he did. This was Mandy. He'd dated her since basically the day they laid eyes on each other their freshmen year. She was too cute for him, he'd thought the day they'd met at their lockers, directly next to one another, so he'd ignored her, too shy for even a hello. He loved the way her red curls bounced when she walked, and the way her teeth flashed just so when she smiled that melting smile and the way her hair smelled like apples. He'll never know why, but she squeezed his hand that first day, said her name was Mandy and she'd like to get to know him. Then, just like that, he couldn't get enough of her. Soon they were spending so much time together they were known as Kandy around the town of Gaithersburg. She called Coach 'Dad' and Kevin's mother 'Mom.' She never missed any of his games and he tried his best to feign interest in her cheerleading…well, he didn't know what to call them—competitions, maybe? But he tried, which was enough for Mandy.

As his eyes found the growing mass of a bruise on the right side of her forehead, he felt a pang of guilt yet little was going to wash away his smile on this Saturday morning.

The Prep boys were the number one seed. The girls were the three. Basketball was back in the town of Gaithersburg. Anybody, even those football-crazed maniacs from Quince Orchard, could have predicted the delirium that ensued in Gaithersburg. Playoffs were the subject of every conversation in every corner of town.

At the Dutch Corner, the restaurant that gave players and coaches a percentage off their food depending on how many points they scored the previous night—50 percent off the bill for 50 points, 90 percent off for 90 points and so forth—was mobbed. Every denizen proudly held a copy of *The Gazette*, with a centerpiece headlined: 'Staggering no more: Prep favorites to sweep playoffs.'

By noon, *The Gazette* was already ordering reprints.

Kevin sat down at the table in the corner with Mandy, Timmy, Jocelyn and his mother. Coach's seat, the one at the head of the table, was empty. The void didn't go unnoticed by the Stottlemyer family but it had long since passed that they let it consume them. They held up their milk and coffee and clinked glasses.

"To Coach," Kevin said.

"To Coach," they echoed.

As much as they tried to eat their greasy eggs and buttery toast and fatty bacon in peace, as a family, it was not possible on that particular afternoon. There was Don, the owner of Don's

Automotive, where Coach had taken Kevin to buy his first car, coming in to shake hands and tell him that wow, what a great season those boys had. How about Roy Ferguson, a Prep alum who hadn't missed a game since God-knows-when, dropping by to tell the Stottlemyers that they had been inspiring to him this whole time, helping him get through a few layoffs and family troubles of his own? Under the table, Mandy held Kevin's hand, stroking his thumb and he would occasionally sneak her a kiss between visitors.

"I love you," she would whisper.

"I love you too," he would whisper back, and he truly meant it.

Then Lyla Storm walked in the door, all blonde hair and blue eyes and legs for miles in her gray Prep sweatpants. Kevin didn't know why, exactly, but he immediately shot up from the table. He no longer felt an intense loathing to her, as he had essentially his entire life. They were bonded by tragedy and that one early morning in the gym had forged a relationship nobody else would ever be able to understand or comprehend aside from these two. He wasn't sure he even understood it. Did they like each other or not? Were they friends or not? He didn't know. Maybe she didn't, either.

Kevin's heart went thump-thump as he made his way over to the Prep star. Mandy watched, slightly suspicious, as her boyfriend strode over to the exquisitely beautiful girl at the doorway, but this was Kevin. She trusted Kevin. She did not trust Lyla Storm. At the entrance, Lyla had already attracted quite a crowd around her. They told her congratulations and great game and wow, they can't wait to see her just crush it in college. They made room for Kevin.

"You were good last night," he said, smiling sheepishly. His face flushed as he realized he had a piece of waffle stuck in his teeth. He wondered if Lyla noticed. He knew he shouldn't care, but he couldn't help it.

"I know," she responded, with the smile that had melted just about every male heart in the town of Gaithersburg.

Kevin didn't know what to do. Hug her? They had only done that once, and he didn't really have any other choice at the time, did he? Shake her hand? No. Too formal. High five? Too childish. He stood there quite awkwardly for a beat, until she saved him.

"Take a walk with me for a sec?"

Kevin hoped his face didn't reflect just how relieved he felt that she rescued him from his inner turmoil. They stepped outside and into the cool mid-morning air. Mandy watched them go until they turned the corner and were out of sight and she resumed picking at her eggs and bacon.

The winter was slowly beginning to bleed into spring, and it was a pleasantly warm morning, though goosebumps still raced up and down Kevin's arms as they walked around toward the back of the restaurant.

"Listen, I'm, um, not too good at this," Lyla said. "I've been a bitch to you my whole life. I've been a bitch to basically everyone my whole life and I'm not saying sorry for that, because, I don't know, that's me, I guess. I guess what I'm trying to say is thank you.

You were really the only one I could go to after Tara…after Tara's accident. I'm not going to get all sappy on you but it meant more than you know, OK?"

Kevin pursed his lips and nodded. His palms had begun to sweat despite the weather not calling for such a reaction. His face felt hot. Her lips, gosh her lips looked so red and, well, did they look a bit…delicious? He wondered what they might taste like.

"Sorry, I didn't mean to take you from your family and everything. I just knew you'd be here and I wanted to tell you that."

She leaned in, kissed him on the cheek and Kevin swore she had poured kerosene on his heart and dropped a match on it. Blood rushed through every vein in his body. He could feel his heart drumming in his temples. She spun and walked away without another word, leaving Kevin in a world of jumbled thoughts and wild emotions. Before she turned the corner, she glanced back, where he stood, frozen yet completely ablaze, sweating yet riddled with goosebumps.

"Hey," she called. "Let's kick some freakin' ass these next two weeks."

Then she was gone.

Maryland Christian Athletic Conference Playoff Round 1

Boys

#1 Covenant Prep vs. #8 St. Anselm's

#4 Bishop McNamara vs. #5 Good Counsel

#3 Bishop O'Connell vs. #6 Bishop Ireton

#2 St. Andrew's vs. #7 Gonzaga

Girls

#1 Bishop O'Connell vs. #8 Bishop Ireton

#4 St. Andrew's vs. #5 Bishop McNamara

#3 Covenant Prep vs. #6 Good Counsel

#2 Gonzaga vs. #7 St. Anselm's

CHAPTER 17

Kevin searched and searched his memory but could never recall a time he had seen Stottlemyer Arena so packed. The fire department had assessed the capacity to be 1,500 before it was deemed a hazard. Kevin estimated the gym was verging on close to double that. At the entrance, fans received either a blue or red shirt. The red shirt said 'COACH' on the front and had Kevin's number 0 on the back. The blue had 'PREP' in bold red letters and Tara's, and now Lyla's, number 35 on the back. The Prep fan section, even 20 minutes before the game, was a boisterous sea of both. It must have been a staggering sight to the few from Good Counsel who'd made the trip and were huddled in the visiting corner.

The mass of Prep fans roared in deafening unison when the girls charged out of the locker room, Lyla leading the group, her face an emotionless stone wall of focus. Kevin and the boys team were doing a run-through in the upstairs auxiliary gym when they felt the floor shake from the explosion emitting from the cauldron of noise down below, like a distant earthquake. It was game time and Stottlemyer Arena grew louder when louder seemed inconceivable.

The boys team didn't bother to leave from their spot in the upstairs gym. The result was predetermined: Lyla Storm would not be stopped today. As could have been predicted by essentially everyone, with the lone exception being the hopelessly optimistic Good Counsel fan, of which there were none, she indeed was not stopped: 15 points in the first quarter, 12 in the second quarter. By halftime, Prep was leading by 24 and the Falcons had only scored 12 points.

There was no need for the rah-rah halftime speech or a reminder of what they were playing for. Koontz just let the girls be girls. They celebrated their obliteration of Good Counsel in that first half with laughs and giggles, hugs and high fives. They poked fun at Good Counsel's clumsiness, overall slowness—"They're so slow they make slow people look not slow!" Nadia crowed—and the complete and total inability to put a ball into a hoop. Normally a stickler for these types of arrogant displays of panache, Koontz didn't care. Her girls were finally having some fun. She'd let them.

As the buzzer sounded, reminding them they had two minutes until the start of the second half, they not so much ran as they danced out onto the court, a jubilant bunch returning for another 16 minutes of wonderful destruction, except for Lyla. She idled at the door, waiting for Koontz, a rare, beautiful, perfect smile, pasted on her face.

"Don't play me," she said. On any other day, of any other year, Koontz may very well have fallen over in shock. This was Lyla Storm, maker of every record in Covenant Prep's book, the boastful owner of them all, and this girl didn't want to play in the playoffs?

But of course, this was not any other day nor was it any other year, and Koontz did not fall over. In a year thick with odd events and one tragedy after another, this was a refreshingly normal request. She eyed Lyla, full of curiosity and wonder, though she didn't press the issue.

"OK." She had longed for the day that Lyla matured into a teammate and not just a player. That day was finally here.

"DeDe will get all the reps then. You get to tell her, though."

Lyla stepped out onto the court to an ear-shattering welcome. She grinned. Ever since she was little and her father told her she would be great one day, she coveted that reaction from a crowd. She ambled over to DeDe, who was running through ball-handling drills at midcourt. She essentially had to scream for her teammate to hear her from five feet away.

"Hey, you! You're starting for me."

DeDe's eyes grew as wide as a 5-foot tall girl's eyes could. She pointed at her chest.

"Me?" she mouthed. Lyla nodded. Her face turned red as a stop sign. DeDe dropped the ball and nearly flattened Lyla, squeezing her in a tight, sweaty hug.

"Are you sure?"

It reminded Lyla of the way Tara lit up when she was sent to check-in. Every time, it would be for Lyla, and every time, her friend would hug her tight and tell her she loved her. "Go get 'em, sis," Lyla would say, and she'd swell with pride when she watched her friend pour her heart out. DeDe was not Tara. DeDe played plenty and was rather good at basketball, yet there was still something about sharing the spotlight, the adoration, that Lyla was growing to love.

"Now go drop fifty on 'em."

DeDe did not score 50 points. She made one lonely layup. She may as well have scored 100, from how her smile stretched from one ear to the other. Nadia picked up the scoring slack, running rampant over the hopelessly undersized Good Counsel post players, getting to the free throw line 16 times and making enough baskets inside the lane that it bore a slight resemblance to a practice drill. Koontz didn't even bother to sit in her coach's seat by the scorer's table. She opted to lounge next to Lyla, observing her star player's oddly altruistic behavior, how she exploded in celebration every time her teammates scored and how she fidgeted when the offense wasn't run correctly. Teenage girls. She'd never understand them.

"You're going to make a great coach one day, Storm," she said over the din of Stottlemyer Arena.

Lyla didn't hear her, too busy calling out screens and seeking adjustments for the offense to make.

"You know, coach," she finally replied in a quiet moment, after Prep was up 30 and the fans had relented. "I never thought I'd be this happy, sitting on the bench."

"Imagine that," Koontz said, throwing her arm around Lyla's shoulder. "Lyla Storm, happy for someone other than herself. My little girl is growing up."

Lyla's throat had the consistency of sandpaper by game's end. It hurt to whisper, much less scream, in celebration anymore. She loved it. She was happier than if she had scored 35 and was the center of attention. It was strange, this feeling, but so, too, was this year. This was a good kind of strange and Lyla could not stop smiling.

"Ms. Storm," Koontz said, as they rose to shake hands with Good Counsel. "I believe you have turned a new page."

CHAPTER 18

In a matter of an hour, Jared's house had become a whorl of colors and humanity. Didn't they know they couldn't fit an entire town into a one-story, two-bedroom house?

Covenant Prep didn't care. Jared certainly didn't. If anybody was going to throw an epic party in this town, it would be none other than him.

Both the boys and the girls had won their opening round playoff games and were bound for the semifinals. It was time to celebrate. There was Warren and Nadia, two of the only black folks in Gaithersburg, cheersing their beers and looking at each other in that way teenagers do that can only mean wonderful trouble by the end of the night. Both of them lived right on the border of Covenant Prep, almost an exclusively white school, and Quince Orchard, almost an exclusively black school. They had a choice: QO or Prep. QO, a public school, was football-crazed, state champs nearly every year. They didn't pay much mind towards basketball. That's why Jack Miller and those boys from St. Andrew's pasted them by 40 a few weeks back. Nadia and Warren were raised with a basketball in their cribs. They couldn't bear the thought of playing for such a sad excuse for a high school basketball team. So they chose Prep. But they loved the kids from QO, many of whom lived just three doors down, so they packed Jared's house with those hulking football champions, who cheered and whooped and hollered as if they were Stags themselves at every game, diversifying the crowd both in the stands and the after-parties. Jared, for his part, was too busy funneling that glorious golden liquid down his gullet to care who was ransacking his house. One Bud Light then another, pouring it down, down, down. His vision grew hazy, his speech slurred. His smile poured from his lips like syrup, sweet and slow.

He jumped up on a table, nearly fell, demanded the music be cut off.

"I have someeeething to say, y'all!" he crowed.

Somebody cut the music.

"We're in the semis!" he shouted.

All of Covenant Prep, it seemed, and a large portion of QO, sloppily yelled in that wild way drunks do. The party raged on. By the time Kevin slipped through the back door, at 11 o'clock that night, held up by a family dinner with Timmy and Jocelyn and his mother but no Coach, the house must have been 100 degrees. The minute he stepped inside, sweat began to coat his arms and chest. His red polo stuck to him. He attempted to wade through the masses but with every step came another slurred "congratulations!"

"You did it!" someone screamed into his ear, spilling a juice concoction down his shirt. Someone else shook his shoulder. Another slapped his back.

"Take a shot with me!" someone else shouted.

Kevin didn't really have much choice, the unknown person tilted his head back so fast. Down came the mysterious liquid, which burned as it shot down his throat. It was awful. It was wonderful. Kevin spluttered and laughed. He was handed one drink and then another. The family room had become a gyrating mass of a dance floor. Short skirts. Low tops. Kevin's mind buzzed. Mandy couldn't make it. Studying, she said. The girl was always studying.

His eyes searched the party, looking for a girl with blonde hair and blue eyes and long legs. He knew he shouldn't be looking for Lyla. He grabbed another drink and tilted it back. It was impossible to make out one person from the next. Everyone was packed so closely together, a bunch of drunken teenage sardines.

Another drink. Down it went. He stumbled into the kitchen and found Jared. Two girls clung to his chest, ogling and running their hands over his muscled frame. Sweat dripped off Jared's hair and his eyes bore a wild, unfocused look.

"Kev!" he yelled, raising a beer. "Semis, baby!"

The girls squealed as Jared raised his drink to the ceiling, sloshing drops all over them.

"Semis!" Kevin returned. They clinked cans and chugged. Kevin coughed. Jared kissed one girl and then the next.

"You know, Jared," a girl in a pink tank top Kevin didn't recognize, gushed. "You're known for being a bad boy. You don't seem so bad after all."

"Well, ladies," Jared grinned. "That's 'cause my good is only just good. But my bad, well, my bad is legendary."

He winked at the both of them and they put their heads together, whispering something, and before Kevin could say anything, they were ambling off in the direction of Jared's bedroom.

"Well, he's having a good night."

Kevin knew that voice. His face grew hot. His palms dampened. If he hadn't already been drenched in sweat, he knew a monsoon would have begun making its way down his face. His heartbeat quickened, tripled more than likely. He turned, not realizing how much he had drunk until he nearly fell over in the process.

"Wow," Lyla said, catching him. He liked the feel of her hands on his lower back and stomach, steadying him. He couldn't help but flex his abs just a little. "You've had a few, huh?"

Kevin grabbed the counter for balance, though he wouldn't have minded if Lyla had been the only thing propping him up. He didn't feel embarrassed. For the first time in what felt like a lifetime, he felt electrifyingly alive.

"Maybe."

Kevin's eyes ran up and down Lyla's body. Her blue shirt cut off a few inches above her belly button, clinging to a perfectly toned figure. Kevin wondered to himself how her skin was so tan in the wake of winter until he remembered that this was Lyla, a basketball goddess who looked perfect at all times of the year. Her honey hair was drawn into a tight ponytail, and her eyes had a spectacular blue fire to them that Kevin could not help but find intensely attractive.

"C'mon," she said. "Let's grab a bottle and get out of here. Too crowded. Too sweaty. I've been here five seconds and I'm already tired of hideous guys touching me with their gross, hairy, sweaty arms."

He knew it was a bad idea. Of course he did. That's the thing about bad ideas, though: Sometimes they just seem so damn good.

"Sure."

The word came tumbling out faster than he had expected. Oddly, he didn't regret it. Drinking with Lyla, away from the crowd that had slowly made Kevin a bit claustrophobic, sounded perfect. They escaped into the night, and how beautiful it was.

The cool air sent shivers shooting up and down Kevin's skin and turned his shirt into an icy saran wrap. It was sensational. They eased down the backyard hill, slipping on the slick and cold ground, moving further and further away from the pounding music and towards the stream Kevin and Jared had fished as kids. Lyla grabbed his hand, leading them toward the rock, jutting out over the water, the one Kevin had named Sunny Stone because the only fish he ever caught there were sunnies. They collapsed onto the cool surface and Lyla opened the bottle of something orange. She swigged it, coughed, spluttered, repeated.

"You played really well today," she said through coughs. "I was actually impressed."

Kevin pinched himself, making sure this was no dream or illusion, that Lyla Storm was complimenting another human being and on their basketball skills, no less. Kevin had played well. He only scored 18 points, not an overly impressive number by any means, but he didn't turn the ball over a single time despite playing every minute. He dished out 16 assists, 13 of which went to Jared, who finished with a game-high 32 points. St. Anselm's never stood a chance.

"I guess I played alright." His cheeks flushed. He wasn't accustomed to talking to Lyla away from the basketball court, though he could certainly get used to it.

"Here."

Lyla passed him the bottle and Kevin splashed whatever it was down his throat. It burned deliciously. They passed it back and forth, two high school kids with oversized dreams and even bigger problems. For how long they did this Kevin wouldn't know, though he knew it would never be long enough.

How it happened, Kevin couldn't recall, but he glanced down and his hand was intertwined with Lyla's, and her head was on his shoulder. They were both freezing and neither cared a bit.

"You know," she whispered, "seeing you, how strong you've been with this whole thing, it really helped me. I never really understood you, never even liked you. You seemed like a freakin' weasel. You have helped me deal with…with Tara more than I could ever be able to tell you. I don't know if I should thank you or what, but I just wanted to tell you."

Kevin's heartbeat quickened. It was bitingly cold but his insides were aflame. He decided to say nothing. He reached up and ran his hand through Lyla's hair, which was icy from the cold and the sweat. She sighed.

"I love it when you do that. The first time you did it, at the gym the other day, was perfect."

Kevin had no idea Lyla even knew he had stroked her hair that morning. She looked up, all blue eyes and beauty. She was gravity and Kevin couldn't fight it. He leaned in and put his cold lips on hers, and suddenly everything inside of him was either fire or electricity. Their lips danced with each other's. She kissed differently than Mandy. Lyla's lips worked methodically, a little more aggressive than Mandy, who was so delicate and careful. Lyla wrapped her hand around his head and pulled him tighter and he didn't resist. He pressed his body against hers and they became one tangled mess. He let the bottle slip from his hand, and it clanked down the rock and splashed into the water and neither seemed to notice. They kissed and kissed until their lips were raw and saliva was gone and all the worries of the world seemed to wash away, right off of Sunny Stone and into the stream below.

CHAPTER 19

Kevin and Jared sat in silence next to each other on the Covenant Prep bench, much the same way the rest of the thousands of Prep supporters were watching the unprecedented scene before them.

Bishop McNamara, they of the .500 regular season record and no real talent, had beaten Good Counsel in their opening round playoff game, booking their date with Prep in the semifinals on this Friday night. Upon learning the result, the Stags celebrated as if they had just won the conference title, for they matched up perfectly against the Mustangs.

"Should we spot them thirty points?" Brandon cackled, and they doubled over with laughter.

"I think we should try to dunk as many times as they score field goals," Jared suggested. They howled again. It was to be an easy win, a coaster to the championship where they would inevitably see Jack Miller and the St. Andrew's boys. They had made very quick work of Gonzaga, thumping them by 38 in their first-round game and would likely do the same to Ireton in the semifinals. The championship was an arranged marriage between those Lions of St. Andrew's and the Stags of Prep. Deals were already being struck by local TV stations to broadcast the game. Newspaper reporters asked Kevin and Jared not about the upcoming game with McNamara—a sure win, no?—but about a rematch with St. Andrew's, the team that had eviscerated them just so in the season opener.

At this rate, though, the much-hyped final was not going to be a final at all. For here was McNamara and their quicksilver fast guard, Jamir Rannals, dancing through a listless Prep defense, lighting them up for 13 points in the first quarter. Rannals worked his magic on both ends. He stripped Kevin three times in the open court, taking each back for a layup. Jared pushed him. Coach Snyder screamed. Kevin didn't know what it was. He was faster than Rannals; or maybe he wasn't. He was a better shooter than Rannals; or maybe he didn't have the touch he thought he had. He began second-guessing himself.

Jared was no better. The triangle-and-two defense, catered specifically to shutting down Prep's stars, was working better than even the McNamara coach in the orange and brown tie could have ever dreamed. Coach Snyder did the unthinkable. He pulled Kevin and Jared, starting the second quarter with 70 percent of his team's statistical offensive production on the bench.

Jared kicked the bottom of the bench and followed it with a salty string of expletives a rank or two below a sea captain. Kevin slumped next to him, head down, sweat puddling on the red strip of wood below. He had never felt so helpless on a basketball court. Even last year, when he was without Coach for the first time of his life, he was still on the court, wielding some influence over the game. Here, on this wooden, uncomfortable bench he had never had much time to familiarize himself with, he was rendered entirely moot.

The whistle blew and in went the ball. Rannals brought it up and fired a 3-pointer over Brandon Thompson, too overmatched in speed to play tight enough to cover the deep shots. Swish. Prep was now down 18-10 to one of the most unremarkable teams in the league. Warren bumbled a pass and down the court the Mustangs went, finishing with a layup. Ten-point advantage.

Kevin could hear Jared, his long hair mopped over his face, muttering something under his breath that was surely less than support for Coach Snyder. Kevin felt his foot tapping against the wood. His palms grew sweaty—anything less than a championship would be a monumental failure. A loss in the semifinals to Bishop McNamara would be a catastrophe.

Garrett Kron slashed in from the wing but his layup clanked off front iron. Rannals, seeing a wide advantage and Prep's only two bona fide creators on the bench, walked it up the court.

"He's gonna milk the clock," Kevin spat. He discovered his teeth were clenched, his jaw tight. And milk the clock is exactly what Rannals did. Brandon made a vain attempt at pressuring him but a slick crossover nearly put him on his butt. Rannals backed up to midcourt again. Kevin glanced at Snyder, standing near the scoring table, lips pursed, hands on his hips.

"He don't know jack shit," Jared hissed. Brandon pressed again and again. Rannals evaded him with the ease Kevin would in a driveway game with Timmy.

Jared leapt to his feet and screamed, "Brandon, just freakin' foul him! Foul him right now!"

Snyder whipped his head around in Jared's direction. Brandon looked over, confused and shrugged, a "What do you want me to do?" expression on his face.

"Foul him right now!" Jared screamed again.

Snyder raced to where Jared was standing, putting his nose against his. "Whose team do you think this is, huh? Whose?" Snyder hollered.

The game seemed to pause for a moment. Rannals hung at midcourt, clearly amused as he watched the opposing team's coach fight with one of his best players in the middle of the most important game to date. The refs shared bemused glances with one another. It must have been quite the scene for the fans, too. Jared pushed Snyder out of the way.

"Brandon, foul the freakin' ball handler!" Jared screamed.

Brandon grabbed Rannals's jersey and the refs, bless their hearts, blew the whistle.

"Timeout!" Snyder yelled.

The Prep players—Garrett and Warren, Brandon and Andy and Bryan—trotted over, as confused as a calculus class, to where Jared and Snyder were now warring.

"Who do you think you are, Younger?" Snyder screamed, veins popping, creating a little blue map on his neck.

"I tell you what, coach, how 'bout you sit back down and let the big boys win a basketball game?"

Jared's calm surprised Kevin.

"You clearly don't know shit. So let us run this team."

Snyder began to say something before Brandon cut him off.

"Coach," he began, almost in a whisper. "I mean, why don't you just hear him out? Nothing we've tried has worked so far, right? Might as well give it a shot."

Kevin was shocked to hear Brandon speak. He was never much of a vocal kid, not on a basketball court at least. He wasn't the most talented or basketball-intelligent on the team, so he had usually left the vocal leadership to Kevin, Jared and Coach.

The veins in Snyder's neck eased their way back to wherever they had come from. He took a deep breath.

"Alright, then, Younger, what's this grand idea we just absolutely have to hear?"

The scorekeeper blew the horn, signaling the end of the timeout.

"Alright, boys, here's the lineup we're going with!" Jared yelled, a maniacal grin on his face. "It's me, Kevin, Brandon, Warren, and Garrett. We're gonna play a box-and-one on Rannals. Kevin, that's you."

Kevin smiled. He knew where this was going. It was the same strategy he and Jared used on the blacktops growing up to beat kids far bigger and older, whose size didn't quite match their intelligence or speed. Which was why Jared wanted Garrett to play instead of Bryan. Bryan was lanky and smooth, with a silky shot and a nice presence for rebounding, but he was slow. Garrett was spry and blindingly fast, a 100-meter state finalist who could play defense like nobody's business. His offense wasn't necessarily excellent, and for a guard he had awful ball control, but his value on defense, in situations like this, greatly outweighed his lack of offensive abilities.

"Kevin is going to force Rannals into the corners. Every time he nears a corner, we trap. Leave your guy open, I don't care. Every other kid on this team freakin' sucks. We're going to kill them. Let's go dominate."

It wasn't difficult to sense that something changed. The Prep players wore wild smiles and looks in their eyes that somehow flashed hot and cold at once.

162

"You sweethearts fixed your little squabble?" Rannals sneered at Kevin. "Mommy and daddy fighting again?"

Kevin smiled. This was going to be fun.

Kevin allowed the entry pass into Rannals, angling his feet to force him left, his off-hand. He pressed and Rannals took the bait, trying to drive past Kevin, but Kevin's legs were fresh from the bench. He was too fast for Rannals, angling him off. As soon as Rannals took a step back, Garrett, with all that speed, sprung like a viper. Rannals backed up again, and again, trapping himself between the defense and half court, exactly how Jared had designed it. He jumped and threw a careless pass across the middle, the very pass Jared was waiting on.

Jared snatched it out of midair and sprinted headlong down the court, all by himself. He loaded up and slammed a tomahawk dunk, and it's a wonder how the roof didn't blow off, the Prep fans hollered so loud. They were on their feet now, chanting and screaming, taunting and jeering. Stottlemyer Arena had turned from docile to hostile in a single possession.

Rannals turned it over again, then again, one more time for good measure. The trap was working better than any of them could have hoped. Jared pulled up for a jumper at the elbow and then dunked another and half the place must have temporarily lost their hearing. Kevin knew he did. It would take until the next morning for the buzzing in his ears to stop. The trap wasn't just effective; it was downright demoralizing.

"Let's run this score up, boys! Leave no freakin' doubt!" Jared screamed, as loud as his throat could muster.

They verged on barbaric, those Stags of Covenant Prep. They hooted and hollered and ran the lead all the way up to 35 points with six minutes left in the game. Rannals turned it over 12 times, not to mention the dozens of others coughed up by his teammates, before his coach finally pulled him, his magic drained entirely. Snyder emptied the bench as well, calling Jared and Kevin over to sit with him, though he left in Garrett, who was having the game, and time, of his life.

"You boys listen to me, and you listen well, you hear?" he said, eyebrows furrowed, forehead creased. Those were the first words he had said since the timeout. Even at halftime, he simply sat with the team, smiling with the comfort of a coach sitting on an 18-point lead and a team playing like jackals. It had been something of a watershed moment, ceding some of his power to allow some insight from his players. Not only that, but it had worked!

"What you two did tonight, you especially, Younger, was damn incredible. This win is yours. You earned it, and I apologize. I was stubborn and angry. I'm incredibly proud of y'all. Listen, I know I ain't perfect and ain't never gonna be, OK? I know I have a lot to learn here as a head coach. Today, I learned a valuable lesson—to trust the opinions of my players. I thank you for that."

He held out his hand and they both took it.

Jared felt a tingle of something inside of him. It was respect, something he hadn't felt for anyone since he played for Coach.

CHAPTER 20

The mustache tickling Mike Storm's upper lip seemed to take on a life of its own. It twitched and trembled. It seemed angry, until you took a look at the man attached to that quivering strip of hair and suddenly a mustache moving seemingly by its own power appeared quite normal. Mike's face was turning curious shades of red as he ripped through that day's *Gazette*.

"Ridiculous," he spat at the headline.

Lyla flinched.

"Honey..." her mother, Sue, began in her languid voice.

"None of that right now."

Lyla toyed with her mashed potatoes and chicken. Sue's fork clinked audibly over her half-eaten salad—no dressing. Mike was breathing heavy now, the anger that appeared to be stemming from his mustache beginning to traverse throughout the rest of his body.

"How many times do I have to tell you, Lyla?"

He slammed the paper in front of Lyla, sending her plate crashing to the floor, decorating the walls with mashed potatoes and gravy. Lyla glanced at the headline she had read dozens of times already. She had actually felt quite proud of it: "*Storm quiet, Blake sets records in Prep win.*"

"Go ahead, Lyla, remind me how many points you scored."

"Dad..."

"Don't you 'Dad' me. How many?"

"Eight."

"Eight! Eight points. Eight. Stinking. Points. What in the world were you doing?"

"Dad I..."

Lyla wanted to be honest. She had never felt so bewildered in her life. She had scored eight points, sure, but Prep had won. Won by 18, to be exact, a comfortable margin by any measure, let alone a semifinal game that most would expect to be at least somewhat close. Truth was, she didn't need to score.

The girls had played Gonzaga. The Eagles were fast and spry, a run-and-gun team who could catch any number of teams off-guard if they had the press working. They were also small, their tallest girl standing 5-foot-6. Nadia, all of 6-foot-4, resembled more a giant than she did a high school teenager when Prep played the Eagles. All week, Coach Koontz had designed plays for Nadia, mostly isolation sets that would give her a one-on-one matchup that Koontz predicted would result in either free throws or a layup. Coach Koontz was right. Nadia went out and scored 24 in the first half, all from right under the basket. While the Eagles were busy double-teaming and trapping Lyla, even when she didn't have the ball, Nadia stood virtually uncovered in the paint. If Gonzaga's strategy was to force someone other than Lyla Storm beat them, which appeared to be the case, Coach Koontz and Lyla were welcome to allow it.

Lyla didn't take so much as a single shot in the first half. She stood in the corner every single possession and yet two purple-clad Gonzaga defenders would come dutifully running over, eager to shut down the best player the state had ever seen. Lyla wasn't even sure they were aware of the score—did they seriously not realize they were down 20 in the third quarter and Nadia was shooting almost 100 percent? She found she rather enjoyed clobbering an opponent without needing to break a sweat.

Evidently this did not sit as well with all of the Storms.

"Do you know what eight points will do to your average, Lyla? Do you?"

Mike was up now, pacing, stomping all over what had been left of Lyla's chicken and potatoes that had been discarded to the floor during his first tirade.

"I tell you what, it's that Coach Koontz. She's never wanted you to be the best. She's always been out to get you..."

Lyla could feel her face getting hot. She grinded her teeth, gripping the table so hard her knuckles turned white as the bone that lay under the skin.

"Always looking for someone else to get the spotlight. She's lucky she has you or she wouldn't win the game."

Sweat was beginning to trickle down Lyla's cheeks. Sue continued to clink her fork against her bowl, toying with leftover strands of lettuce.

"I tell you what," Mike said, lowering his voice to a whisper that dripped with venom. "I hope you score sixty points in the championship—and lose. That'll show her, huh, sweetie?"

Lyla lost it.

"Are you freakin kidding me? Are you serious?"

Oh, this was some storm that had been brewing inside of Lyla Storm. It was a hurricane, a tornado, a tsunami of rage and anger and fury. Lyla's nostrils flared and hands shook. Her eyes flashed an icy cold and the most menacing of expressions formed on her face. Her voice lowered, almost to a whisper, which had a rather chilling effect.

"We win, kill a good team by eighteen points and you sit here, all you can think about is me—me, me, me. That's all it's ever been about, which means it's really about you, you, you."

She was close now, up in her father's face, finger jabbed squarely in his chest.

"All you care about is my stats, my points, my this, my that. Just so you can go tell all your friends about your Alllllll-Americannnnnnn daughterrrrr, the one you raised and taught the game and blah blah blah. You wanna know the truth? Do you? Truth is, you didn't teach me jack squat. The only thing you taught me was how not to act. You know what sucks? I didn't even realize this until Tara died. I didn't realize what a selfish asshole I was because I was trying so hard to impress you, to be you, to make you happy. I was so concerned with who you wanted me to be that I didn't even know who I was. My best friend had to die for me to learn this? That's freakin' despicable. I'm ashamed of myself and I have you to thank for that. When I look back at how you had me act since I first picked up a ball, I'm freaking disgusted and you should be too. We could lose every single game one-hundred to ninety-nine and all that would matter to you is if I broke some record. You know what? That's what I thought, too. All I wanted was to score. All I wanted were points, attention and stupid newspaper articles to hang in my room. Because that's what you wanted. All I've wanted is to be just like my dad, because my dad was sooooo proud of his little girl. You know, I don't care about that anymore because that's not basketball. If I wanted to be some superstar individual, I'd play some stupid sport like golf or something but that's not basketball. Look at the box score again, dad, and tell me the final score of the game."

Mike paused, unsure if the question was rhetorical or not.

"Do it!"

Not rhetorical.

"Sixty to forty-two, Lyla."

"That's right. Do you know how many we beat them by when we played them in the regular season? Do you?"

Mike remained quiet, silenced by the storm in front of him.

"We won by twelve and I scored thirty-six. I was the one who told Coach Koontz to use me as a decoy this time. It wasn't her idea, it was mine. I told her to use Nadia more. I knew Nadia would get single-covered by a girl like, I don't know, four feet shorter, if she was even covered at all. I knew they'd put two girls on me after the way I played against them the first time. So guess what? That means we're playing four-on-three, with an insane mismatch in the post. That means there's pretty much no possible way we're not going to score. Even if Nadia missed, we'd have an uncovered girl, maybe Brittany or Gabby, in there for a rebound. So yea, it was my idea. Mine! Not Coach Koontz's. Even if it was her idea, I would have agreed with it.

"But all you see is the headline, the one with my name and 'quiet' next to it. You don't see that we're even in the finals and that we won the game. We won, dad. Won. As in, we beat the other team. As in, your daughter can win a championship, and you can go tell all your buddies about it, and how Prep won another title because you raised your perfect little basketball player. You just care about you, the same as you didn't care that one of my best friends died. You didn't even go to her funeral for crying out loud! All you wanted to know was when I could play basketball again, when I could make headlines again, when I could get another scholarship offer, when you could brag about me again, when you could begin living through me again. I'm done with it, dad. I'm done with you."

Lyla snatched the newspaper out of her father's hand and ripped it clean in half.

"Here's your stupid freakin' paper. Hang that up on your stupid freakin' wall."

Then she walked out the door, not knowing where she was headed but wherever it was, it had to be better than this place.

CHAPTER 21

Kevin was face down on his bed, phone right next to his pillow, which was fast becoming damp with tears. It had finally happened. Had to be done. He called Mandy, told her everything. About Lyla. About the kiss. She had reacted as he expected, though no mental preparation could ever block the pain from hearing his girlfriend of nearly four years burst into uncontrollable sobs.

What had she done? Why her? Why, of all people, was it Lyla Storm? Was she better? Was it because she played basketball? Mandy wasn't good enough. She knew it, just knew it.

Kevin was silent as she rained down the barrage of questions and accusations. The lump in his throat kept him from speaking, and he knew if he tried, he would melt into a sobbing, sad excuse of a boy. So he let her vent, and as she wailed, his mind rewound, all the way back to their first date, first kiss, first everything.

It rewound to the day she was flying back into town after a missionary trip to Peru. He picked her up from the airport with two dozen roses and a 1,000-watt smile and the only thing brighter than his grin was the one he got in return from that beautiful girl with the bouncing red curls. She collapsed right into his arms and he knew he was deeply in love right then and there.

It rewound to Valentine's day his sophomore year and the disaster date that ensued, when his beaten-up Sable broke down on the side of the road. They made the best of it and had a pizza delivered directly to his car on the side of the road. And so they sat, two high school kids, young and in love, sharing pepperoni pizza in a broken-down car, on the side of the road, on Valentine's day, mopping up the grease that spilled down their faces with kisses.

It rewound to every basketball game, when he would open his locker first thing in the morning to be greeted by cookies or brownies or any other of his favorite treats. Mandy would bake them all herself, writing "good luck" or "go Prep" or "I love you" in blue and red icing.

God, what had he done? Here was Mandy, 18 going on 26, bright and stunning and full of this unbridled zest for life, who had never so much as argued with Kevin. Perfect, really. Here was

Kevin, who had been moody and mercurial, unpredictable as the weather, and he chose...Lyla? Lyla, who was simple like quantum physics. Lyla, who Kevin could not have disliked more if he tried since the day he laid eyes on her. Lyla, who boasted and bragged and was seemingly everything Kevin hated most. Lyla, who was—who was quietly slipping into his room, striding across his blue carpet with those long, perfect legs. Who was pulling back the covers of Kevin's bed and sliding in next to him. Who was putting her arms around his stomach and laying her head on his chest. Who was turning his heart to wax and melting it one thunderous heartbeat at a time.

Suddenly, Kevin's mind was blank. Suddenly, his heart, which had felt dead and heavy as an anchor not a minute ago, was alive, racing, thump-thumping so hard he could feel it in his ears. Suddenly he was...happy? Excited? He didn't know, he just knew that one girl had just made his whole world go upside down and inside out.

"Hey," she whispered, kissing his ear. Funny what one word can do. His busy mind went blank. Heart erupted into flames.

"Hey." It was stupid. It was all he could manage.

"Were you crying?"

"Might have been."

"Why?

"Mandy."

"Oh. Sorry."

"Are you?"

Against his ear, Kevin thought he could feel her lips curl into a smile. She kissed him again.

"Maybe," she whispered. "Probably not."

She kissed him again.

He shouldn't have wanted to hear those words, shouldn't have been hoping to hear those words, shouldn't have turned over to his side, so he was facing that stunning girl and returned that kiss. Yet he sure did want to hear those words, he sure did hope to hear those words and he sure did turn over on his side and plant a kiss smack on her lips, and he sure as hell didn't regret a single bit of it. Eventually, he was able to pull his face away from hers, though it was one of the more difficult things he had done in a while. Tougher, he regretted thinking, than the phone call with Mandy. He was, after all, quite curious about Lyla's arrival in his bedroom at 9:30 at night.

"What are you doing here?"

"Long story."

"Can I hear it?"

"Only if you want to."

"Sure."

"Just my dad. He sucks."

"What did he do?"

"Told me I was terrible because I only scored eight points, that Nadia was selfish because she led the team, that he was going to get Coach Koontz fired for it."

"Wow."

"Yea."

Kevin knew Mike Storm. Well, he didn't know him, but he knew of him. Everyone in Gaithersburg knew who Mike Storm was. He had seen him at all of Lyla's games, though the man had been kicked out of no less than five for berating the refs and Coach Koontz had even banned the guy for two games last season because he threw a full soda can on the court, which promptly exploded, over a bad call.

Neither of them said anything for some time, to the point that Kevin thought that Lyla, with her steady, rhythmic breathing, might have fallen asleep.

"I wish I had your dad," she finally whispered.

Kevin felt a jolt in his heart and his hand reflexively reached for the angel wing tattoo on his chest.

"You miss him, don't you?"

"Every day."

"I was always jealous of you. You know that? Of your family, your parents, your dad, even you and Mandy. I really was."

Kevin could hardly believe the words he was hearing. Lyla Storm? Jealous of him?

"You're funny, Ly."

"I'm not kidding, Kev."

Kevin did think about it, though, and he began to understand. He did, in his mind, have the best dad in the world, which was quite the contrast from Lyla's. He did have the most supportive mother he could ask for, whereas Lyla's was—well, Kevin couldn't recall he had ever met Mrs. Storm. Timmy could be a bit much with all of his energy but Kevin was his hero. What older brother wouldn't want to be a hero? Then there was Jocelyn, and if Jocelyn wasn't the sweetest thing on the planet, he wasn't sure what was.

"It's getting late, I better go. I'm not sure why I came here at all, honestly. It's not like we're dating. Sorry. Sorry I messed up you and Mandy."

Truly, Lyla was sorry, not for what happened, only for the way it did. She didn't really care about Mandy's feelings but she still had a sense of morality.

"We have the championship tomorrow. Better get some sleep."

Kevin's heart sunk. He wished she could stay, to calm his mind before the storm that awaited the next night, in the state championship against Jack Miller and St. Andrew's. He knew she couldn't, though. Mom wouldn't allow it. Speaking of that, what did she think of Lyla's late night visit? He hadn't told her about the breakup with Mandy. The whole school knew about his and Lyla's midnight trip to Sunny Stone. Had word spread to his mother? Did he care?

She began to get up but Kevin grabbed the collar of her shirt and gently pulled her back down, so her lips were on his again and the electricity coursed through his veins. Lyla smiled her heart melting smile, kissed him on the forehead and slipped out the door as silently as she came.

CHAPTER 22

There they sat, the 12 Stags of Covenant Prep, lost in that place teenage boys go before they're about hurl their bodies about in the biggest game of their lives.

The locker room deep inside the bowels of the University of Maryland's XFinity Center smelled of sweat and socks and teenage boy, but none of them would notice such a simple thing as the scent of a locker room. Not now, not two minutes before tipoff, when they would be asked to shut down Jack Miller, whose only accomplishment to date was being the best player the state had seen in decades. No big deal, right? They had just watched Miller drain 25 straight 3-pointers without so much as a blink of the eye. He smiled and grinned as easily as if he were lazing through a November post-practice shoot-around.

In that locker room, though, the Stags were deep in reflection, taking a flashlight to their souls, inspecting themselves for what they would need to bring home a state championship.

Kevin and Jared were inspecting their souls as well, though not quite as deeply as Brandon, whose feet were a blur of frenetic tapping, or Warren, who was staring so intently at a ball it looked like he may have thought all of the answers he would need over the next 32 minutes were locked somewhere inside its leather. Garrett jumped rope, his breaths coming out sharp and purposeful as a boxer's—*"ssst," "ssst," "ssst."*

Jared, well, Jared was being Jared. He was sprawled across a bench, back propped up against a locker, and it appeared he didn't have a single worry in the world. For all Kevin knew, he could have been napping. Kevin had so many worries on his mind he may as well have had nothing on his mind, sort of like a lightbulb in a thunderstorm: Sometimes there's so much electricity it just goes 'pop,' and suddenly all goes completely dark. He wanted to clear some space, to sift through the jungle of thoughts polluting his mind, so he walked past the fidgeting Brandon and stone-faced Warren, past the languid Jared and Coach Snyder, so deep in his notes and clipboard he didn't notice Kevin strolling past at all. Kevin stepped out of the muggy, swampy locker room and into the cool concourse, breathing in gloriously frosty air.

"Hey, bud."

Jack Miller, he with the perfectly-toned muscles gleaming with sweat, stood outside the St. Andrew's locker room, twirling a ball in his hands. Had it been anyone else standing outside their locker room, alone, twirling a ball in their hands just minutes before the state title game, the biggest game of his life, Kevin would have thought them nervous. Of course, this was not just anyone, this was Jack Miller, and Jack Miller, as Kevin knew, or presumed to know, did not get nervous.

"Not getting ready with your team?" Kevin asked. What a stupid question.

"Naw, man, I always take a minute to myself. Too much nervousness in there, man. I just wanna ball, you know? And besides, I was actually hoping to catch you before the game, man."

Kevin gave him a sideways look. He'd never felt the need to talk to anyone on the other team before a game.

"Listen, man, I just wanted to let you know that I feel for y'all, what y'all have been through. I respect the hell out of you for playing and all and for making it all the way here. That's real talk, man."

Jack extended his hand and Kevin took it.

"Appreciate that, Jack."

"Play well, man. Gonna be a fun one."

The buzzer sounded from the gym. Game time. Jack nodded at Kevin, Kevin nodded at Jack, and both returned to their locker rooms with the unspoken agreement that would be the last of their pleasantries over the next 32 minutes.

Brandon still tapped. Warren still stared. Garrett had dropped the jump rope for sit-ups. Jared still may as well have been asleep.

"Alright, boys," Kevin called. Where he found the steadiness to bellow he had not a clue. "Let's go take home state."

The enormous wall of red seats behind the far hoop was the first sight to greet Kevin as he charged out of the hallway and into the cavernous, beckoning arena. Kevin had never played in a place so big: 20,000-person capacity. Of course, not all of these seats were filled for a high school basketball game, state championship or not. The state championship was played every year at the University of Maryland, home to one of the biggest arena's in all of college basketball. It was quite startling to a high school player who was accustomed to 1,500-capacity shacks.

The Wall, as the mountainous pile of red seats directly behind the hoop was called by Maryland students, was closed off, making for a nightmare of a shooting background. Kevin found it easier to shoot with screaming and whooping and waving fans behind the hoop rather than an armada of empty red seats, stretching higher than any high school gym ceiling. It was on that very side that he missed two straight free throws last year and lost the state title. In their shoot-around earlier that afternoon, he had taken 100 free throws and only made 70. He shuddered. The silence, the stillness, was unsettling to him.

The Prep fans were dressed in red, matching the seats. As had become the norm since both teams began playing again, all the males wore the shirts with "COACH" written on it and the females with "FRENCH" and her—and now Lyla's—number 35 on the back. They all stood, all howling with the enthusiasm one would expect from a couple thousand high schoolers bent on bringing home a state championship.

As Kevin sprinted around the court in Prep's customary lap, he felt something he hadn't felt in some time. His stomach seemed to flutter, kind of like that feeling you get when looking down at the peak of a roller coaster, knowing a dive is about to happen and your heart will land somewhere between your chest and throat. It's strangely exhilarating and mortifying all at once. Kevin loved it. He smiled as he hit mid-court and slammed the ball down on the giant 'M' logo in the middle. Nerves were good. This felt right. Prep's 11 other players gathered around, linking arms in a circle around Kevin, beginning to sway back and forth, first slowly then picking up speed with each one. Kevin clapped his hands, looking each player in the eye and yelled,

"Who are we?"

"Prep!"

"Who are we?"

"Prep!"

"What are we gonna do?

"Win state!"

"What are we gonna do?"

"Win state!"

"Brotherhood on three, boys. One, two, three..."

"Brotherhood!" the team yelled.

They all clapped and whooped, a bunch of champagne bottles shaken, bubbling to the brim, ready to burst. There was a huddle around Coach Snyder, some pregame introductions. The ref called for captains and said a few sentences. Sounds. There were no sounds, not really, at least. It was almost as if the refs were trying to speak to Kevin underwater. Hands were shaken. Kevin couldn't recall any specifics of anything that had just transpired. His mind was racing too fast. Someone was watching a movie on his life and kept flipping between fast-forward and slow motion. He couldn't think, couldn't feel anything, aside from all these gosh darn butterflies. His mouth was dry yet his hands were coated in sweat.

Then a man dressed in black and white stripes was tossing the ball into the air and Warren was jumping. That ball was being slapped in his direction and, suddenly, he was moving, his legs reacting on instinct alone, his arms doing the same. Suddenly, his hands were cradling the ball and the Prep fans erupted as if they had just won the game. The noise brought Kevin back, back from whatever alternate reality his nerves had taken him to and onto this massive court with 31 minutes and 59 seconds left of basketball to play and a state championship on the line. Kevin allowed himself a breath, another breath, a big, deep, lung-stretching breath before taking his first dribble.

The Prep fans were on their feet, jumping, pounding the seats, chanting— "Let's go Prep!" (clap, clap, clap-clap-clap). The place was pure, unfiltered kinetic energy. Kevin coasted down the right side, Miller giving him two steps of space to do so, then swung it to Brandon Thompson, who flipped it to Jared on the wing, and into their shuffle offense they went. Kevin cut sharply off a pick set by Warren at the elbow but Miller was right behind him. Jared demurred, waiting for Bryan to roll around on the second pick of the offense. His man was late, getting caught up by Warren's giant pick and Jared hit him on the left elbow for an easy jumper.

Swish.

Explosions from the Prep fans. Encouraging claps from the St. Andrew's faithful.

Game on.

Miller raced up the court, catching the Stags off-guard, which shouldn't have happened given the dozens of hours of film they watched on the Lions. They were guard-heavy and fast-paced. Where they lacked in size they made up in speed and tenacity. They knew this. Yet Kevin was still a step late in his attempt to close out Miller at the 3-point line and he slid around the right edge, out-angling Kevin to the baseline, beating Warren by a mile to the hoop. He laid it in with no more trouble than he would in the driveway by himself. Kevin spat, disgusted, and called for the ball. Warren flipped it in and Kevin was off to the races but Miller was there, smothering him at half-court, where he was joined by a teammate, trapping Kevin. He heard Jared call for the ball and he swung it wildly over the middle, precisely where the Lions wanted him to throw it. A St. Andrew's forward stepped in front of the pass and jogged in for a layup.

"Kevin!" Coach Snyder screamed, not so much out of anger, but in an attempt to simply be heard over the raucous crowd. Kevin glanced over. "Slow the ball down. Play our game."

He nodded. Coach Snyder was right. He had fallen into St. Andrew's' trap. They encouraged teams to push the ball, to play their game. Speed wasn't a weakness of Prep's, but it wasn't their greatest strength, either, whereas it was the reason St. Andrew's was nearly unbeatable.

Warren tossed the ball in and Kevin held it for a beat, eyeing the Lion defense. He knew they liked to shift defenses on most possessions, flipping from a 1-3-1 to a man-to-man to a 2-3 zone to a three-quarter court trap to a box-and-one as smoothly as if they had been playing it the whole game. They were a brilliantly coached team and it took a cerebral point guard to beat them. It was chess, not checkers, as Coach liked to say, when you played St. Andrew's. Kevin was about to test his chess skills.

Jack and a teammate idled near mid-court, suggesting a trapping defense. Kevin slowly walked the ball up, dissecting the defense for the weakness, for each one, he knew, had a soft spot. As he moved up, Jack and his teammate slid back into a 2-3 zone. Kevin grinned.

"Triangle!" he called. It was a play designed for Jared, a double-screen on the baseline that would delay the back-right defender in getting to Jared, who would be open for a corner three. As soon as Kevin stepped over mid-court, Jared began looping off the wing towards the baseline, where Warren and Bryan had slipped down, setting the double-screen. As soon as the screen was set, Bryan flashed back up to the elbow, posing the threat of another easy jumper, which drew the top defender toward the middle. With the defender at the bottom of the zone still fighting through Warren's pick and Bryan occupying the defender at the top, Jared was left wide open, as always, in the corner.

Swish.

Five to four, Prep.

And so it went, this chess match between Jack Miller and Kevin Stottlemyer, Prep and St. Andrew's, a town that needed basketball to survive and a town that simply loved little more than to watch its boys play basketball.

Jack's next points came on a spinning jumper on the wing, giving St. Andrew's a 12-11 lead. Oddly enough, it was Brandon Thompson and Bryan who were doing the scoring for Prep, as the Lions, though shifting defenses, were clearly attempting to minimize the impact Kevin and Jared could have. At the end of the first quarter, St. Andrew's led 15-13. Kevin and Jared combined for just five points, while Jack accounted for eight of the Lions'.

"Hell of a quarter boys! Hell of a quarter!"

Coach Snyder still had to scream, the place was so loud. St. Andrew's' fans were the only ones who could rival Prep's. Like Prep's, they hadn't sat since the opening tip, and the close of a quarter would do nothing to change that. Prep's thousands bounced up and down on the bleachers, a rhythmic drumming that turned deafening when the black-clad crowd from St. Andrew's did the same.

The blood in Kevin's veins ran hot and wild. His heart thump-thumped against his temples and his hands shook with that blend of nerves and adrenaline that athletes crave. He smiled, couldn't help it. This was what he lived for. He reflexively touched his angel wing tattoo and glanced up at the sky, knowing this was what Coach had lived for, too. The buzzer sounded, cutting off Coach Snyder mid-speech. Kevin hadn't heard much of what he had been saying, other than to keep doing what they were doing. One of the pieces he caught was that Snyder said eventually, at some point, Jack Miller had to miss. Physics demanded it; no athlete could sustain shooting at that rate for an entire game, against such a solid defensive team. Problem was, sports aren't played on paper and percentages don't often make the leap from the stat sheet to the court or field. Jack Miller was not missing at all.

A floater in the lane kicked off the second quarter, which preceded a 3-pointer and a pull-up on a fast break. Snyder switched Jared onto him, hoping his extra size might keep him contained, but Miller drove right past, drew Warren to play help defense, and dished it to a wide-open Lion under the hoop. In three minutes, Prep went from down two to down 10.

"Kevin, dude," Jared said after another Miller jumper. "What do we do? He's unreal."

Kevin shrugged. He really didn't know.

"Not much we can do, I don't think. Let's just keep this thing close until he cools down, alright?"

They did, mostly because Brandon Thompson was playing out of his mind. It was inexplicable, really. He was, somehow, matching Miller essentially shot for shot. St. Andrew's had gone to a triangle-and-two for the entire quarter in an attempt to shut down Kevin and Jared. Miller, being a supremely talented defender, was having his way with Kevin, forcing him to get rid of the ball almost as soon as it was in his hands. Jared was just cold. He had turned the ball over twice and missed a few open jumpers, though the important thing was that he was getting them, for it was only a matter of time before Brandon cooled and Jared regained his form. How long Miller could keep his pace up was anybody's guess. He had done it all season. It wasn't that Brandon couldn't sustain his strangely torrid streak, it was that such a workload had never been demanded of him, and Kevin knew the clock was ticking.

Then, with the Stags losing 36-28 with two minutes left in the first half, the clock hit all zeroes on Brandon's hot spree. Jared drove baseline, drawing the closest defender down for a double-team, which left Brandon open at the top of the key. His shot missed everything, beckoning a serenade of "Airball! Airball! Airball!"

chants from the St. Andrew's side. Brandon's face flushed. He wiped his hands on his shorts.

"Don't worry about it, brother," Jared said on his way down the court, slapping him on the butt. But Brandon did worry about it. He lost his man on defense and Miller hit him for an easy layup. On the next possession, he threw the ball three rows deep in the stands in an attempt to find Kevin with an ill-advised cross-court pass. Kevin glanced at the clock, 45 seconds left in the half. Prep just had to survive. The wound was open, the Stags just had to limit the bleeding. Problem was, they were being attacked by the best basketball player in the state of Maryland, and Miller knew exactly what Kevin was thinking.

He pushed the ball up the court, firing a pass to Brandon's man, who took a hard dribble to the baseline and pulled up for an easy jumper.

Swish.

"Press! Press!" Miller called.

Miller sprinted toward Kevin, denying him the ball. Jared's defender, a lanky and deceptively fast kid named Chris, did the same to Jared. The Lions were forcing the ball to Brandon, who was ice cold and freaking out, or Bryan, who could hardly dribble up the court without a defender, let alone a trapping press. Warren, knowing even a visibly shaken Brandon was a better option than Bryan, tossed it into Brandon. It went right through his hands. Brandon's man scooped it up and hit a quick layup. Thirty-eight seconds left and the press was still on.

Coach Snyder was screaming something. The Lions' fans were roaring. Kevin's mind was racing. Brandon was in an all-out panic.

Warren went to Bryan this time. He bumbled the pass but controlled it enough to square up and face the court. Brandon's man was charging over to trap him, so he flipped it back to Brandon who, thankfully, caught the ball and headed up-court. His man reversed course and attempted to steer him toward the corner but Brandon had evidently found his wits and beat him to the middle, creating a three-on-two with him, Kevin, and Jared, who went streaking up the sidelines the moment they saw Brandon catch the pass in the middle.

They had done this drill no less than a million times in practice. Brandon, in theory, was supposed to drive down the middle until a defender committed to stopping him, which would then leave either Kevin or Jared open for a layup or an easy jumper. Brandon, in the scrambled state that he was, passed early to Jared on the left before he even hit the 3-point line, eliminating a huge chunk of the advantage of a three-on-two. Jared took one dribble left, feinting towards the baseline, and made a hard crossover back towards the middle. Chris, his defender, nearly fell from the abruptness of the move and was beaten. Miller, who had stuck with Kevin, didn't even bother to help. He wasn't stopping Jared. Nobody was stopping Jared.

Jared took one more dribble and rose, up, up, up, higher than Kevin had ever seen his friend jump. He cranked his arm back as far as his shoulder would allow and slammed home as violent a dunk as Kevin had ever witnessed in real life.

Kevin's ears were still ringing when he took his seat in the locker room for halftime. He had never heard such a noise in his life. Prep's fans had exploded into delirium after Jared's dunk, slamming the bleachers, screaming until they could scream no more, clapping their hands, dancing and losing their collective mind. Miller had missed the final shot of the half, sending Prep into the locker room down a manageable 42-30. They had done the only thing they could have—survive.

Had a passerby dropped in the locker room at halftime of that state championship game, they would never have known the Stags were down 12. They whooped, hollered, screamed and high-fived. Jared's dunk had ignited something inside of them that had been dormant. Perhaps it had simply released the jitters that invariably accompany a game of such magnitude.

It didn't last.

The problem with energy, you see, is too much of it can be an issue. The same energy that can light a city can also cause it to be draped in complete darkness. A surge of it, not unlike the one charging through the Prep locker room, can be as detrimental as it can be beneficial. Where Prep was all freneticism and jubilance, St. Andrew's was a model of equanimity. The Lions didn't let the late push from the Stags bother them. In fact, they appeared not to have noticed at all.

Miller was surgical once more at the start of the third quarter, slicing through the lane, finding holes in Prep's defense that were self-induced. The Stags were crazed, a bunch of adrenaline junkies on a high. Brandon overran passes, going for steals he shouldn't have, creating five-on-fours and mismatches all over. Warren was jumping out of the gym—on pump fakes, which left the basket wide open, which is not how a team wins a state championship basketball game. Even Kevin and Jared found themselves victim to the wild momentum swings. Jared tried to dunk twice more and missed both, crashing to the floor in a heap of tangled limbs and hair. Kevin tried to break the press alone, by dribbling, not trusting Brandon or Bryan with the ball and, certainly, not Warren. Turnovers ensued.

The third quarter was as disastrous as the closing of the second was marvelous. St. Andrew's only scored 13 points in the frame. Prep managed just four. More than the added nine points to the deficit, though, the Stags were gassed. All that running and jumping and flying about had winded them, to the point that Garrett and Andy were seeing more minutes than they had in any game all season. Even the Prep fans seemed to have dwindling energy supplies, for they hadn't so much as yelled, screamed, stomped or jumped the entire quarter, not that the players could blame them. There wasn't much to cheer about, was there?

"Calm down!" Snyder yelled in the huddle before the start of the fourth quarter. "This is not Covenant Prep basketball! This is not how we have played all year! This is not how we have practiced all year! Kevin, Jared, you guys see anything out there?"

Kevin shrugged. He really didn't know. Jared stared at his chair, sweat puddling below him, and it was unclear if he had heard a word the entire break. His mind was somewhere, but this colossal gym was not it. The buzzer sounded and the Stags took the court for their final quarter of the season.

Time. It wasn't on Prep's side.

They were down 20 with eight minutes to play. No force on heaven or earth could stop time's inexorable march, ticking down the minutes of Prep's state championship hopes. The comeback was slow: a layup here, a 3-pointer there. But it was almost always offset by a St. Andrew's score. Five minutes and change were left and Prep was down 17 when Jared had one of his signature surges of crazy. He rebounded an errant shot and took off down court, so headlong Kevin didn't even bother to follow. He knew that look. Jared, for better or worse, was going to do this one himself. So he went, racing past one defender and then another, until he was just outside the lane with two defenders converging on him. Up he went, arm raised back for a dunk that was sure to shake the gym. Only problem was those defenders, who went up with him, crashed into Jared in midair and down they went together, a mess of arms and legs.

Kevin blinked, frozen. Had he heard what he thought he did? Was that audible crack some sick joke from his imagination? Couldn't be real, not now, not this game. It didn't take long for Jared to confirm it was no joke. He writhed on the ground in pain, all veins and strained muscle, gripping his right leg, which was bent at such an odd angle Kevin thought he might hurl from the sight. Whistles blew and the game stopped. It took the breath out of the crowd in an instant, a gust of wind to a candle. All was silent except for Jared's groaning and hissing, which Kevin knew for sure to be an imaginative string of curses that many in the crowd had likely never heard before. Kevin felt a hand on his shoulder, Coach Snyder. He ushered him over to his fallen teammate, under the basket, surrounded by nine young men kneeling on one knee, all eyes pinned on Jared.

"Shit, that hurts, bro," Jared said through clenched teeth. "Did I at least make the freakin' shot?"

Coach Snyder put a reassuring hand on his shoulder and smiled.

"'Course you didn't, you out of control animal. I don't even know if the ball stayed in the gym. But, boy, if it wasn't the most spectacular attempt at a missed dunk I've ever seen. I'm not even mad. That's a move I don't even think Michael Jordan would have tried."

Jared laughed and winced.

"Easy, Jared. Stretcher is on its way. Just relax."

Minutes later Jared was strapped to the stretcher, helplessly being wheeled off the biggest game he'd ever play.

"Kevin," he said, waving him forward. "Come here a sec."

He held out his hand, and when Kevin took it, he pulled him in close, so close that Kevin's nostrils stung with salt and he could see a white layer of dried saliva forming around his teammate's mouth.

"This is your game. Yours. I don't care how good Jack Miller thinks he is, or how bad we're losing right now, this is yours. I know this year has been some shit for you but you have to take this. This is what your dad has prepared you for since you could walk, dude. I'm not talking about winning. I'm talking about bringing those guys together and pulling off something that most right now consider to be impossible. You're all those guys have right now. You're all I've had for a long time. These next five minutes are yours. This is for your dad, for Prep, for Gaithersburg, for Tara French. You've helped save this town, Kevin, whether you like it or not. So go finish the damn job and bring me back a state championship trophy so I can show all the girls and get laid all the time."

Kevin nodded and embraced Jared in an awkward hug, for how exactly are you supposed to hug a guy on a stretcher, you know?

"Love you, bro," he said, letting go of Jared's hand before turning and facing the court. It was time to go to work.

Kevin took stock of his teammates, who were scattered like shrapnel. Brandon stared absentmindedly at the court. Bryan studied his fingers. Garrett toyed with the ball. Warren was taking in deep breath after breath, as if he might have a heart attack any moment.

"Boys!" Kevin called. "On me."

The crowd was whistling and clapping for Jared as he was wheeled off the court but Kevin could barely hear it. Ten sets of eyes peered at him and he knew from their empty gazes Jared was right— he was their only hope.

"Listen," he said, "this is a game, right? That's what people tell us anyway. Our teachers say it's not as important as homework. Our parents say it's not as valuable as good grades. Our newspapers say it's just a game, but look at what we've done, boys. Look at what we've done for this town. Without this team, I'm not sure this town makes it through this year. Without this team, I'm still in a dark, dark place. My family would be in a dark, dark place. Y'all saved my life. Y'all saved my family. I want you to know that. If people think this is just some game then fine, let them, but we all know it's so much more than that. So let's go show them what we can do with a game. By the time these next five minutes are up, I don't want a single one of you to be able to stand. I want you to be bruised, sweaty, bloody, out of breath, exhausted. I want you to know you did everything in your power to win this game. If we do that, boys, there's no way we lose. For Coach."

Kevin put his hand in the middle of the huddle, and one by one they piled on top, until it was just Coach Snyder left.

"Coach on three, gentlemen. One, two, three..."

"Coach!" they yelled in unison.

They came out of the huddle an outburst of determination so mechanically precise it seemed to come directly from the gates of heaven rather than the realm of human kinetics. There was Kevin, knocking down a 25-foot 3-pointer. There was Brandon, knifing through the lane for a layup. There was Bryan, hitting that sweet elbow jumper he loved so much. All the while St. Andrew's grew tired, lazy, complacent with a lead that seemed untouchable. Even

Miller threw away a pass and Chris traveled once and missed two bunny jumpers that would have fallen with ease earlier in the game. Suddenly, the lead was down to 10 with 1:45 to play, then four with 45 seconds and Prep, this machine of perfect and flawless basketball, couldn't be stopped. It came down to Kevin and Miller. Had to. The Basketball Gods would have it no other way. Miller broke the press and idled at midcourt, waiting to be fouled. There was Kevin, smothering, hands in a perpetual blur of motion, yet a careful blur, for he knew a foul would send Miller to the line for essentially two automatic points.

A gift.

It came in the form of a fingernail. Kevin's grazed the ball as Miller crossed over, and it knocked it off course just so, catching Miller's foot and careening out of bounds. Prep ball. The Stag fans were red in the face, voices surely shot. They hadn't quit screaming since Jared was carted off, and surely not a single one had sat. The noise was nothing compared to the volcanic roar that followed, when Kevin rose up and buried a 25-foot fadeaway 3-pointer.

One-point game now and St. Andrew's was in an all-out panic. It must have been Christmas morning, for there was another gift. Chris threw a hurried pass to the center, who looked open enough at midcourt but that happens when Warren is on defense. It's a part of his trap—give his man some space to bait the pass that is to come then spring that 40-inch vertical and unfurl those breathtakingly long arms and snare it. For that's just what he did.

Now the ball was in the hands of the most careless player on the court and Kevin was wheeling back to help.

Three seconds left, he took a handoff from Warren.

Two seconds, he dribbled down the sidelines, where Miller and another defender were angling to cut him off.

One second.

A crossover, back to the middle.

He had them beat, toasted.

Then there was a foot, hooking onto Kevin's as he cut. Now he was tumbling to the ground, the ball bouncing, ownerless, into the middle of the lane. There was the buzzer. Kevin slammed against the floor. Hysteria and confusion abounded. St. Andrew's celebrated wildly while Prep's faithful roared in protest.

Nobody had heard it, the whistle. The ref had called the Lions for tripping. Kevin would shoot two.

One to tie. Two to win.

This was the place that had haunted Kevin's dreams. He had been here, just last year, in this very same situation. He had looked over to the bench, where he knew he wouldn't see Coach but expected, needed, him all the same. Coach, of course, wasn't there. He was in an operating room, and only Kevin and his family knew. Kevin had missed both shots on this line that day. He'd watched as Jack Miller and St. Andrew's stormed the court, taking state right out of Kevin's hands.

And here he was again. No Coach.

It's a soul-searching place, the free throw line. Just you and a ball and a hoop. No defenders. You miss, it's entirely your fault. You make it, and the glory is all yours. Here Kevin was again, inspecting his soul, searching for Coach. Coach would know the right thing to say, the exact words to whisper into Kevin's ear to get his shot just right. Kevin wasn't sure he needed Coach anymore, though. He had done this for the past year. He could do it one more time.

"Player, are you ready?" called the ref, looking at Kevin.

Kevin nodded. He'd have spoken, but he couldn't. Mouth was too dry. All the saliva had disappeared the moment he stepped up to the line. Where it had gone, he had no idea, because he was so damn thirsty his throat felt like it hadn't had any liquid poured down it in days.

The ref bounced the ball over to him, and the bounce echoed in the cavernous arena, which had turned into a vacuum of 10,000 fans holding their breath. He cradled it, inhaling, once, twice, one more time. He eyed the hoop, spinning the ball in his right hand. There was that wall, that dreaded mass of red seats. He ignored it. Just look at the back of the rim. It's the only thing that matters. A flex of his knees, two bounces with his left hand, one more spin in his right then a new addition to his free throw routine: He cradled the ball in his left hand and kissed his right, planting it overtop his angel wing tattoo on his chest. He smiled, suddenly, strangely, at ease.

Then the shot was up and, oh, it felt so nice. Kevin held his release, pure as snow, and the ball ripped through the net in a swish.

The Prep fans exploded and then hushed immediately, for this was not yet over. Kevin couldn't believe it, but he felt a smile pulling on the corners of his lips, and then he was laughing. This was fun. This was what basketball was meant to be. He was just a little kid in the driveway again, shooting hoops with his dad.

After the first, there was never any doubt in Kevin's mind he would bury the second, just as there was never any doubt in his mind he would miss the second in last year's state final. The ref passed the ball back and through his routine he went: spin in the right, two bounces with the left, spin on the right, kiss the tattoo, shoot.

It was even cleaner than the first. Before the scoreboard could even flash the final score, 74-73, the Prep students were bursting out of their seats and onto the court, mobbing Kevin. His teammates pulled his jersey. Hugging. Everyone was hugging, screaming, smiling. Kevin had never seen so much happiness on one half of a basketball court.

"We did it!" Brandon screamed in his ear, shaking his shoulders. "You did it!"

Someone kissed his cheek. Someone slapped his chest. Someone tackled him to the floor. Someone picked him up.

He had never felt such a rush of emotion. Adrenaline coursed through his veins. His cheeks hurt from smiling so big. Hot tears ran down his face as he hugged one person to the next, pushing out of the half-court scrum. Somehow, Jack Miller had found a way to fight through the crowd, coming face to face with Kevin.

"You're a hell of a player, Kev!" he said, screaming into his ear. "What you did with this team, man—you deserve it. Proud of you, man."

He hugged him quick and tight and bounded off. Kevin smiled, watching him go. His brain forgot about the students, the fans, the championship, the free throws. In that moment, Kevin was just a boy who wanted to be with his mom and little brother and sister.

"Mom!" he yelled through cupped hands, searching the stands. "Tim! Jocelyn!"

If there were ever a moment a teenage boy needed his family, this was it. His eyes, which he discovered were thick with tears, scanned and scanned until they found that unmistakable Lion King backpack down by the scorer's table. His mother had wisely kept Jocelyn and Timmy from rushing onto the court, in fear of them being crushed by the stampede of Prep fans. Kevin sprinted as he had never sprinted before, diving into a hug with his family. The tears he had cried before hadn't been much at all, for now he was outright sobbing, body shaking, and he couldn't have cared any less.

"I love you guys so much!" he said through the sobs.

"Ew! You stink!" cried Jocelyn, squirming out of Kevin's grasp, and they all laughed.

Kevin's mother kissed him on the cheek.

"Salty, too," and they all laughed again.

"We're so proud of you, Kev. So proud. Dad is proud too, prouder than he's ever been of you."

Kevin nodded.

"I know," and he wrapped his arms around his family one more time, closing his eyes, wishing the moment would never end.

CHAPTER 23

The place was quieter than the dead. Ever been in a 20,000-seat arena so silent you can hear the sound of the fellow in the upper deck chewing a hot dog? You shouldn't. It's awfully discomforting. It felt like a vacuum in that gym, so many people held their breath.

Lyla's shot, the 3-pointer she heaved as time expired with Prep down two, wasn't just a shot. No, this was the very substance of life of Gaithersburg. This was what defibrillated a pulse back into a community that saw that very thing taken from them twice, one at an age far too young, the other from a man many thought might very well be immune to that tricky thing called mortality.

Lyla's shot tumbled end over end, a perfect backspin rotation, just like Coach Koontz taught her since the girl could walk and first discovered that she could pour her life into an orange ball. Just there, standing in the tunnel because they couldn't bear to sit with the rest of the Prep fans, were Mr. and Mrs. French. They didn't much care if the shot went in or rimmed out. They had witnessed a town mired in tragedy rally around a basketball team that would have thrown in the towel weeks ago had they not put it back together. Their little girl couldn't be there, inevitably sitting on the bench—no, Tara would certainly be standing in a moment like this, too excited to be confined to the prison of a seat. She would be screaming 'til she was purple in the face and her voice turned into an odd squeak of a thing. Her legs would almost be as tired as some of the players' legs. She refused to sit with such a steadfast resolve that Coach Koontz eventually gave up and stopped barking at her to please, for the love of God, just sit down. Yet Tara was there. She was in those t-shirts, the red ones that read 'FRENCH' on the back. She was in Lyla, the brash-turned-humble girl nobody seemed to know what to make of anymore.

And there was Lyla, tumbling down, down, down, crashing to the hardwood below, a defender draped on her like morning dew to grass. There would be no call here. Ref couldn't decide the championship game like that. No way. Not enough contact. It was up to the ball and the shot fired by that girl looking, pleading, with it to just go in, lying next to two girls who were pleading for it to just do the opposite.

Prep had come too far for it to end this way. They had met an O'Connell team on the wrong day, when its two sisters, Megan and Katie O'Brien, the ones tangled with Lyla on the court and begging the hoop to spit out just one final shot, had such hot hands that, at some point, it seemed as if they were spewing actual fire. Fourteen times they shot 3-pointers and watched them drop, and even Coach Koontz, she of the implacable demeanor, had no answer.

"Keep playing defense!" she had urged her Stags, only for one of the two sure-shooting sisters to do it again. The rest of the team had done nothing; Megan and Katie had combined for 50 of the team's 52 points. O'Connell's reliance on individual talent wasn't all that unlike Prep's, who had used 32 points from Lyla to stay within striking distance of the Knights. Nadia had shown up somewhat, scoring 10, and DeDe managed to put a few buckets in, but that was about it. It was Nadia and Lyla vs. Katie and Megan while six other girls sort of roamed about, the magnitude of the game enveloping them, rendering them essentially useless in any competitive context.

Lyla was used to this and Nadia was beginning to become accustomed to it as well. The sisters were no exception—O'Connell wouldn't have scored 10 points in any game without them and they were the only team to give Prep a game the entire season, or at least when Lyla was playing. The Stags had beaten them by four in their first meeting and the sisters had scored 38 between them. Lyla could only cover one of them and DeDe and Gabby, fast as they were,

were not purebred basketball players and couldn't match the sisters skill for skill. Nevertheless, Lyla would guard one while the other torched one of the Stags then Lyla would switch and the other would catch fire. It was the only team in Coach Koontz's extensive memory to ever stump her as a coach; she simply didn't have enough pieces to play the chess match. But she had Lyla, the ultimate equalizer, and it had worked out quite well over the past four years.

It was close now, the shot, just a foot or so away from the hoop. Kevin peeked through his hands, which were covering his face, too scared to look. Jared, sprawled out over a few seats, his casted leg propped up, gripped Kevin's arm so hard Kevin had lost all feeling in his forearm and hand. Not that he cared. Feeling would come back. This shot was eternal.

The ball hit back rim and bounced straight up. Shrieks from the crowd. The bubble of quiet was beginning to burst. It clanged front rim. Lyla lay there, helpless. She heard Katie whisper "Don't do it!" and Megan hiss "No way!" And for the first time since she dribbled a ball, her immediate basketball fate was out of her hands, up to the rim and the Basketball Gods she swore right then and there she'd pray to more if they could just...let...the...ball...go...in.

Side rim.

Mike Storm was on his knees, clutching the seat he had fallen out of in an attempt to stand up too fast. This was it, the future of his girl. State champ. Hero. It was destiny. No way the ball could miss. No chance it would roll off the rim.

Yet it was rolling now, spinning precariously on the right edge of the rim. Only the hopelessly optimistic could have thought it still had a chance and on this night, there were thousands of hopelessly optimistic fans. The ball slipped off the rim and fell, a soft thud of leather on wood, and for a brief moment, it seemed time was standing still, the split second between when you see a firework go off and when you hear the sound.

Then it came. The O'Connell fans detonated with a mighty cheer. They charged the court, a whirring mass of blues and whites tripping over one another, celebrating. They jumped at midcourt and hooted and hollered just like the Prep fans did for the boys, and why shouldn't they have? They had just beaten Covenant Prep, one of the most storied girls basketball teams in the state. They had just beaten Lyla Storm, the girl the papers deemed a Goddess on a basketball court. Unstoppable, those stories read. Well they had just moved the immovable object, right off the top of the standings, and they were going to celebrate accordingly.

Katie turned to her side, facing Lyla. She knew Lyla well enough. They had played against each other since they could walk. She had never really liked the girl, because how could she? Lyla was a snooty braggart who had beaten Katie's teams senseless since they first played one another but she respected the hell out of Lyla Storm, and Lyla sometimes showed some respect to her. Just this year, Lyla had forwarded Katie and Megan an email from the LSU coach, who was inquiring about other players in the area. Lyla had written down their names, noting that she had never seen girls who could shoot like those sisters and passed along the LSU coach's info. An unspoken friendship had bloomed from the rivalry. At that moment, Katie knew no words were the best words for her new friend, so she hugged her instead and then she was off, jumping into her fans' adoring arms, hooting and hollering like the state champ she was.

Kevin's hands remained firm on his face. Jared's grip loosened on his arm, hanging there, limp. The Frenches stared at the jubilation and dejection before them, unsure of what to do next. Mike sunk further onto the stairs, tears welling in his eyes. Coach Koontz remained kneeling, hand covering her mouth, frozen in a gasp.

Kevin was the first to move. Every attendant from Covenant Prep seemed paralyzed from the result. He rose, hopping the guardrail and onto the court, striding to where Lyla lay, crumpled in a heap, hands over her face, her body shaking from the sobbing. He collapsed right next to her, cradling her head, stroking her hair. He was a player; like Katie, he knew no words could soothe an athlete after a loss, much less one who had missed the game winner in the championship of a season that meant far more than just basketball. He didn't speak. He just laid right there with her on that court as the Prep faithful gathered themselves and made their way down to say goodbye to the players. Out they went, one by one, dejected fan after dejected fan, making their way for the exits. One by one they would stop by Lyla, begin to say something, and freeze. What could they say? Kevin just shook his head. There was nothing to be done, not yet, not for some time.

This was an athlete who had just gone from the peak to the cellar in a single shot. They squeezed her shoulder and walked on to their cars that would take them back to Gaithersburg. They all left, even the delirious mass of O'Connell fans and players, until it was just Kevin and Lyla and a janitor mopping up the confetti and dirt and sweat and tears that remained on the court.

"Kev," she whispered. "I failed."

It was the first words she had spoken in what seemed like hours. Her voice, scratchy and dry, sounded foreign, empty, far from the exuberant girl who had once loved nothing more than talking trash but now whose love for her team was uneclipsed.

"No, no, no, no," he whispered back. Kevin placed a kiss on her forehead and she snuggled her head even tighter to his chest. "You didn't fail at anything, Ly. Think about it. Think about this season. You could have—some people even thought you should have—given up the day Tara...the day Tara left. You could have just packed it in right there and y'all could have forfeited the season. Nobody would've blamed y'all at all. But what did you do? You played. By God, y'all played. You see what you did to this town? You saved it. We, the basketball teams, saved this town."

"Think so?"

"'Course I think so. I know so. How else would people have moved on? How do you think I moved on? How my family moved on? We used basketball as a lifeline. It was the only thing that bonded us together. It was the only thing that bonded this town together. Without basketball, Gaithersburg would have been a really bad place, Ly. Without basketball, Jared drinks his face off every night. Without basketball, some people have nothing good left in their lives. This was it for them, for me, for you. It doesn't matter that you missed that shot. It matters that you put yourself in a position to shoot at all. We gave them something to have hope in.

"They could see us playing after what we went through, and they could say 'Hey, if they can make it through that, why can't I?' And so they did. All because we played a game, Ly. That's it. Nobody is going to judge you, or anybody else on that team, for missing one daggum shot and not winning what, like you're nine-hundredth championship in a row? No, the only thing people are going to remember is that basketball saved this town. You saved this town."

Lyla looked up and opened her eyes, and Kevin thought he might never have seen something so beautiful in his life. She was a teary-eyed, sweaty, stinking, raggedy mess, but boy if he wasn't deeply in love with that sweaty, stinking, raggedy mess.

"I love you."

"I know."

Kevin couldn't help but laugh. Lyla.

"Now that's the Lyla I know. C'mon, let's get out of here."

He went to stand up but Lyla grabbed his arm and pulled his face next to hers, so her lips were on his ear.

"I kinda love you too."

Kevin's smile could have lit up the gym.

"I know."

For the first time since that shot rolled off the rim, Lyla Storm smiled.

"Let's get out of here."

He pulled her up and they walked down the tunnel and out into the cool black night, back to the town they'd saved through a game.

CHAPTER 24

Kevin wasn't sure why he rose out of bed at that same hellacious hour.

The alarm howled at 5 o'clock in the morning as it had every morning throughout the basketball season and, just as he did every morning, he flipped over and pounded it and sat up in bed. He didn't need to, of course. The basketball season was over. A four-foot high trophy, gleaming a whitish gold hue in the moonlight from the window, stared back at him as proof.

Yet he got up anyway—couldn't explain it. It was just something he felt he had to do, a visceral need to see the court one last time—a goodbye, of sorts. Closure—to the season, to his high school career, to his final year ever able to look in the stands or bench and see Coach.

A yawn escaped his lungs and he let out a long exhale, watching as his breath plumed in front of him. It was mid-March but it was still cold in the mornings and evenings in Gaithersburg, before the sun could burn through the fog and frost. He didn't bother to pick up his gym bag. Kevin knew he wouldn't be doing much shooting or running around. He was just seeing an old friend.

He slipped quietly downstairs, out the door and into the refreshingly frigid morning. The cold air always felt nice on his lungs, like a gulp of ice water during a fourth quarter timeout. No cars were on the road quite yet. It was Saturday, after all.

As he expected, the Prep parking lot was vacant and Kevin pulled into his normal spot.

He hurried up the pathway to the gym. Cold air only felt so good for so long before goosebumps riddled his arms and tightened his muscles. He pulled the hood of his sweatshirt snug over his head and jogged to the double-doors he had opened every morning for roughly the last 180 of them.

The gym was its same, dusty self, just the way Kevin liked it. The only thing missing was the ball rack. Kevin guessed Coach Koontz had finally locked it up. There was no way she could have expected Kevin to still show up to shoot at this ungodly hour with zero games left in his high school career and no real reason to be there at all. Kevin wasn't mad. He didn't much feel like shooting anyway. Even the coach at Towson, where he had verbally committed to play, advised him not to touch a ball for a while. Best to take a rest, both mentally and physically. He just sat down at midcourt and closed his eyes, allowing a film of memories to play on the back of his lids.

He thought of Coach, teaching him how to shoot a jump shot when Kevin was three and how Kevin cried and cried and cried when he discovered he wasn't yet strong enough to heave it all the way up to the hoop.

He thought of his first game in a Prep uniform and he actually laughed out loud. Kevin had tripped running out of the tunnel.

He thought of Jared and their odd, winding relationship throughout these past four years and how it had ended with them as state champions, brothers, and future Towson Tigers. It wasn't all that much different from most brothers, really—the fighting, the bickering, the unequivocal love, whether spoken or not, that kept them bonded.

A sound broke Kevin's thoughts.

The door. Couldn't be.

Kevin spun on his butt and there, standing at the doorway, inexplicably, was Lyla Storm.

She wore her normal getup: blue Prep sweatshirt, red Prep sweatpants, stunning as ever.

"You too?" he said.

She shrugged.

"Just felt right for some reason. I don't know. Can't believe it's over."

She glided across the gym floor and sat down cross-legged next to Kevin, resting her head on his shoulder. Kevin kissed her on the top of her head and a whiff of peaches and strawberries filled his nose. He inhaled. He loved her smell. In fact, he realized, he loved basically everything about Lyla Storm.

"Weird," was all he said, lowering his voice to a whisper.

Kevin wasn't sure how long they sat there, leaning on each other at midcourt, much the way they had leaned on each other the past month. Perhaps it was hours. Maybe just minutes. Eventually, Lyla, who Kevin was sure had drifted off to sleep at some point, broke the silence.

"Wanna get breakfast?"

"Yea. I'm starved."

"Where ya wanna go?"

"Dutch Corner. Duh. The boys team gets fifty percent off until next season for winning state."

"You're buying then."

He laughed and stood up, knees creaking and aching, the standard symphony of post-season wear and tear. Lyla reached up, waiting for Kevin's hand to help her up. He pulled her into a kiss instead.

"I love it when you do that," she said, kissing him once more.

"Me too."

She stood up, and hand in hand they walked out the door, and neither glanced back at the empty gym.

Acknowledgements

I could write a thousand books and I doubt I'll ever know where to begin when it comes to acknowledgements. There are so many people to thank, and not nearly enough words on this page in which to do it. But there is one thing for certain: I will forever be indebted to my parents, Jim and Jill, whose unequivocal, unwavering support of their prodigal middle child will never cease to astound me. Everything I've achieved thus far is a direct result of how you two have raised me, Tyler and Cody.

Speaking of those two, I must acknowledge my two brothers, whose support for me and the pursuit of my dreams is eclipsed only by my parents.

To my first line of editing defense, Alex Cook, I must thank you for your honesty and also for your wonderful ability to light up a room, even if that room is filled with a frustrated writer, an overweight Rottweiler, and crappy beer.

To my high school basketball team and perfect little town of Hampstead, Maryland, which provided more inspiration than I expected for this project.

To all of those who have helped me along my writing journey. There are far too many to mention, but in particular, I will remain eternally grateful for my University of Maryland professors George Solomon and Marlene Cimons; the Northwest Florida Daily News squad Brandon Walker, Seth Stringer, Devin Golden, Skip Foster, William Hatfield; all in California who have deemed my freelance work worthy of publication, particularly Brian and Don Patterson.

And, of course, to my lovely, absurdly patient girlfriend, Lakaylah, who would have much rather been binging on The Office but instead was dealing with God knows how many questions of "Which word works best here?" "Does this make sense?" "What if I put this here?" "Is this not the worst thing you've ever read?" "I should probably scrap the whole thing, right?"

Writing is without a doubt the most frustrating undertaking a person can bring upon themselves. It takes someone a little bit unhinged to write a book...and then find the crazy in them to write another...and then another. So here I acknowledge all of those who have written books, and continue to write and inspire and move and stir something within readers they didn't know they could feel from ink on a page.

www.ingramcontent.com/pod-product-compliance
Lightning Source LLC
LaVergne TN
LVHW051048080426
835508LV00019B/1767

* 9 7 8 0 6 9 2 8 8 5 2 8 4 *